The Black Knight

An African-American Family's Journey from
West Point—a Life of Duty, Honor and Country

Clifford Worthy

Front Edge Publishing

For more information and further discussion, visit
TheBlackKnightBook.com

Cover photography by Jordan Buzzy
www.JordanBuzzy.com
Cover design by Becky Hile
www.RadiantPunch.com

Published by
Front Edge Publishing, LLC
42015 Ford Road, Suite 234

Front Edge Publishing specializes in speed and flexibility in adapting
and updating our books. We can include links to video and other online
media. We offer discounts on bulk purchases for special events, corporate
training, and small groups. We are able to customize bulk orders by adding
corporate or event logos on the cover and we can include additional pages
inside describing your event or corporation. For more information about
our fast and flexible publishing or permission to use our materials, please
contact Front Edge Publishing at info@FrontEdgePublishing.com.

In Atlanta in 1932, Patsy Louise Worthy took her son
Cliff, age 4, to a photo studio for this formal portrait.

To the memory of my mother Patsy Louise Worthy,
my son Mark Eric Worthy and first wife Lillian Elizabeth Worthy.

Contents

Praise for *The Black Knight*

Academy graduates are special, and Cliff Worthy is definitely one of those special people. He has fought his way through virtually every stage in life with his faith in God giving him the necessary strength and courage.
Rick Forzano, former Head Football Coach of the Detroit Lions, the U.S. Naval Academy and the University of Connecticut.

~

In this authentic story of one man's life journey, we are given a glimpse of the true struggles on which faith and commitment are built. Cliff Worthy reminds us what it is to be human—as a soldier, as a husband and in his important role as a parent. As father of three remarkable children, it was the life and specialness of his son Mark that led him to dedicate his time and his wisdom to the Angels' Place mission—helping to provide homes and hope to hundreds of individuals with developmental disabilities.
Cheryl Loveday, Executive Director of Angels' Place and the Honorable James L. Ryan

~

It is with great pleasure that I recommend Cliff Worthy's book, *The Black Knight*. Having followed him a decade later, I know the contribution he made to the Academy recognizing that we minority cadets lead to a more successful Army. We officers who followed him and the hundreds of minority cadets at the Academy today appreciate his tremendous contribution.
Joseph B. Anderson Jr., West Point Class of 1965

First and foremost, Cliff Worthy is a good soul.
Rich Homberg, President of Detroit Public Television

~

Colonel Worthy's understanding of and commitment to the highest standards of soldier systems continues to be the cornerstone of professional excellence in America's Army!
Bruce G. MacDonald, Major General, U.S. Army Reserve (Ret) and former Vice President, General Motors Global Communications

~

Congratulations on delivering your distinct and meaningful journey. I admired you as a cadet-teammate in our Academy days—now I know "the rest of the story." Well done!
William R. Richardson, General, U.S. Army (Ret) and former Commander of the United States Training and Doctrine Command (TRADOC)

~

Stories of certain lives deserve to be told and preserved. They serve as inspiration for all of us and for generations that follow. Colonel Cliff Worthy's is one of those lives. The Black Knight is his story. It is uplifting to learn what this man has experienced, accomplished and now shares with us.
James B. Hayes, former Publisher of FORTUNE magazine, former Chairman and CEO of Junior Achievement Inc.

Foreword

By former U.S. Rep. John Dingell Jr.

This memoir of retired Col. Cliff Worthy may seem like the story of one family, but it really is the story of many American families. Cliff's story reminds all of us that—at our best as Americans—we are called to help each other build a stronger, healthier community. America's great strength is that we come together here—we come together in all of our wonderful diversity, reflecting our families' origins in places around the world.

My own family is Polish-American. I'm proud to be Polish and to have grown up with a deep appreciation of family and friendship surrounding me. What's so inspiring about Cliff's story is—just as in my Polish-American heritage—those values of family and friendship were the foundation stones in Cliff's African-American family. My grandparents came from Poland. Cliff's grandparents came from the South. We all wound up in Detroit and are proof of the strength that comes from the vibrant mix of cultures and races that is the life's blood of Detroit.

My father, John Dingell Sr.—who played a crucial role in the life of the Worthy family—was a wonderful teacher to all of us. He taught me what it meant to truly be a public servant. As I followed him into Congress, I never forgot what he said: "We are servants. We are not masters of people. We serve—and that is the highest calling of all."

Dad was a courageous, remarkable man! Even before he ran for Congress, Dad was committed to helping other people. He believed that working people should come together to help each other through unions. He got very active in Democratic politics. In fact, he was one of the few really strong Democrats in an area and a time when he sometimes seemed to be virtually alone in that. Then, he was hit with tuberculosis, and he refused to let that stop him! At one point, he even went off to Colorado where the doctors thought he would die of TB. Instead, he fooled all the medical people and recovered. He came back to Michigan in 1928; he ran for Congress in 1932; and began to serve in 1933 as President Roosevelt came into the White House.

Dad was proud to be part of all that and served until he died in 1955. Dad really was a philosopher and a visionary. He understood that America is greatest when we all work together. Racism and all the savagery that has been resurfacing in the last couple of years should have no place in our America. These hateful appeals that try to tear people apart along lines of culture or creed or class are striking at our foundations as a nation.

I was a U.S. Army veteran attending Georgetown by the time President Truman signed his historic order in 1948 to integrate our Armed Services. I had spent two years in the Army during World War II and had a couple of near misses. I was supposed to go into the Battle of the Bulge, but I got meningitis, so I wound up for two months in a hospital. I was supposed to be in the first wave to invade Japan. I had my orders to go when President Truman dropped the bomb that ended World War II. In each case, I was ready to follow my orders and go.

In Cliff Worthy's story, I am inspired by that same commitment to service. While I served in the Army for a relatively brief time, Cliff carried that courageous commitment through many years from the Cold War to Vietnam.

What moves me about his story is that, wherever he went, he carried with him the inspiration of my father's decision to send Cliff to West Point as a cadet. That was the kind of thing Dad took pride in doing. That was one way Dad could show others the possibilities of what all Americans can achieve. Dad opened doors for people. He certainly opened the most important door in Cliff's life.

Today, as Cliff and I both are in our 90s and have retired from public service, we share our pride in family. We can see those around us continuing in this courageous vocation of service. We need to keep opening doors for other families. If my father had not taken that chance in the 1940s of sending a young African-American student from Detroit to West Point— Cliff would not have had his remarkable career. And, as you will read in this memoir, without Cliff's life of service, I doubt that we would have his daughter, Kym Worthy, serving as our Wayne County Prosecutor today.

As it was in the past, our country once again is deeply divided. I love this country. Cliff Worthy loves this country. I hope that this memoir will remind you of what it truly means to be an American.

We come together. We serve.

FORMER U.S. REP. JOHN DINGELL JR. *is the longest-serving member of Congress in U.S. history. He was a member of the U.S. House of Representatives from December 13, 1955, until January 3, 2015. He did not run for re-election in 2014 and was succeeded by his wife, U.S. Rep. Debbie Dingell.*

Preface

By Kym Worthy

You think you know your parents.

In October of 2015, I received a phone call from my dad. He was planning to move from his longtime townhouse in the suburbs of Detroit and was downsizing. He had recently donated his dress gear and other items from his time at the United States Military Academy at West Point to the Charles H. Wright Museum of African American History. The Assistant Curator of the Museum, Jennifer Evans, was thrilled and asked my dad to sit for a videotaped interview to go along with his donation to their archives.

However, there was a little twist. They wanted me to conduct the interview! So, on October 21, 2015, my dad and I sat in the museum for two full hours with Ms. Evans behind the camera. I walked him through his life, background and history. I sat and listened to his stories of the racist South, deciding to forego medical school and matriculating at West Point, and his exemplary 23-year-long military career. I listened to his experiences with rampant discrimination and untold success. I heard stories that I had never heard before. All powerful. All impactful. All mind boggling. Some that had I known earlier may have reshaped in ways big and small my relationship with him.

This was by far the best time that I have spent with my dad. I will never forget it. My relationship with my dad has at times been very rocky—rocky for years at some points. Rocky because I lost my mother when I was 17 very suddenly and I was not in the loop. Rocky at a few other times as well. However, the two hours I spent with my dad talking about his life more than made up for a lot of that. You will read these stories and others in the following pages.

I discovered, among other things, that my father is not really as aloof or dispassionate as I thought. In fact, he is just the opposite. He had been through more struggles than I knew. I understood more about him in those two hours than I did through many years before that.

I have always been proud of him, but when you grow up living the life of an Army Artillery Brat, you think your upbringing is normal. I knew that moving every year to a different state or country, having a Full Bird Colonel for a father, and a stay-at-home mother with a master's degree was definitively not normal, but I was clueless about just how extraordinary my parents really were. You will now know, too.

I have—rather had—two siblings. My brother died suddenly some years ago. I am the middle child. I often wondered whether I was indeed a foundling taken in by my parents because I have always felt very different from the rest of my family. Over time—and in reading this book—I have discovered that this is not true. I am a lot like both of my parents. We really have a lot in common. I am not sure how I feel about that. But I do know this: What they both had to endure is what you read about in books and watch in the movies. I know for sure I would not have handled everything within the pages of this book with as much grace, dignity or character as my dad.

I thought I knew my dad. As it turns out, I did—and I didn't, which is not a bad thing at all. After reading the following pages, you will—and you won't. But you will have a great portrait of what a real American hero looks like. And that is a very good thing.

KYM WORTHY is the elected Prosecutor (District Attorney) of Wayne County, Michigan. She is the first African-American and the first woman to serve in that capacity in Michigan. A former Assistant Prosecutor and Circuit Court judge, she is best known for the prosecution of the former Mayor of Detroit, Kwame Kilpatrick, and her work on obtaining fresh justice for the victims of the untested 11,341 sexual assault kits found in Detroit in 2009.

This photo of my great grandmother Patsy, who began
her life as a slave, was taken in the late 1800s.

Walking Through the Door

Whether you turn to the right or to the left,
your ears will hear a voice behind you saying:
This is the way, walk in it.

Isaiah 30:21

I am not the product of privilege, but I am from solid stock. The values flowing through my ancestral bloodstream are biblically based and, most likely, you will find they are values that flow through your family as well.

I was taught that the road to fulfillment in life is paved by the relentless pursuit of excellence and steadfast trust that God will guide us. As you read my story, however, you will also see that opportunities are sometimes thrust upon us unexpectedly. A successful life depends as much on recognizing and embracing important opportunities as it does on our tireless commitment to a chosen course. Sometimes, despite the plans laid out in front of us, our lives take twists and turns that we never could have imagined. If we are open to change, we can allow Providence to guide us.

In the late 1940s, West Point was virtually out of reach for young men of color. In that era, many colleges and universities had racial barriers and offered few options for poor students, whatever their race. But, in those years, America was changing in surprising ways. A new racial openness at West Point was triggered by direct presidential action. I benefitted from crossing paths at just the right time with Congressional Representative John Dingell Sr., who was committed to knocking down unjust barriers wherever he could. My journey to West Point was not the result of any grand plan that I devised. I barely knew Congressman Dingell existed and he had surely never heard of me as I was growing up—but somehow Providence brought us together at a historic moment. That connection between us, however brief and unlikely, opened up an entirely new path for myself and my family. My openness to that unexpected convergence transformed our world.

In these pages, I celebrate many of the traditional values that are the foundation of families like mine—and perhaps like yours as well. But I also know as a lifelong soldier, father and man of faith that a good life also involves reaching out and taking risks. You will read about some of those daring moments in these pages—like the night I was traveling with my wife around suppertime, walked into a roadhouse in the South to get a couple of hamburgers and instead encountered a very dangerous reception. You will also read about the time that during my training as a new artillery second Lieutenant I boldly attacked a target of opportunity even though I knew that my battery commander was looking over my shoulder and was skeptical that a young black officer could meet such a challenge. I met the challenge. I might have been rattled by his doubtful gaze. I gave the proper commands. The guns roared. That senior officer's eyes were opened just a little more than they had been before.

Ultimately, this book is about daring to walk through doors and face whatever we find there. In your family, you surely have experienced this kind of challenge at some point. As parents, my wife and I walked through the door of raising a son with special needs. We embraced that calling. As an officer, I boldly stepped up to do my job even when my deployments took unexpected turns. Wherever you find yourself in life, you will face new doorways too. This is a book about finding the courage and confidence to open those doors—and walk into the new world beyond.

My story is true as I have documented it and affirmed by the grace of God. This is a story of unlikely triumphs and sometimes overwhelming tragedy. I wrote this account, not because I hope readers will lionize me as some kind of hero, but because I know so many other men and women are struggling along a rocky road toward fulfillment each day. Sometimes ominous new fears loom ahead of us. Sometimes a skeptical gatekeeper doubts that we can succeed and tries to bar our way.

In these pages, I invite you to accompany me as I march with my family through all the challenges life could throw at us. I trust in God that by sharing our stories we may all find strength and recognize that we truly are companions on a journey toward a better world.

My father, Clifford Worthy Sr.   Cliff at age 16.

The matriarch and patriarch of the Colbert clan:
My grandparents Jack and Addie Colbert.

In the 1940s, my Grandmother Addie sits proudly in the middle of this photo with all of her children surrounding her.

I grew up looking forward to these big family gatherings.

My mother Patsy sits lower right with her siblings.

The Village

My mother, father and 14 brothers and sisters sowed love's harvest.
Years after they were all gone, I ate from that harvest when I needed it.

Gordon Parks in *A Hungry Heart*

When I was born, I was wrapped in the dream of my proud relatives that, one day, they would have a doctor in the family.

That dream hung heavy on my shoulders. After all, I was the only child born to Clifford and Patsy Worthy in Atlanta, Georgia. When I was 11, we moved to Hamtramck, Michigan, along with thousands of other black families in the Great Migration toward the Northeast, Midwest and West. The waves of Michigan-bound black migrants settled especially around Hamtramck and Highland Park, small enclaves within Detroit, largely because of Henry Ford's astonishing $5-a-day offer to the world. When he broadcast that offer in 1914, Ford initially drew families toward his factory in Highland Park and later, he drew more immigrants toward the world's largest integrated factory along the Rouge River. Ford hired men of all races and ethnicities, betting that a diverse workforce was a hedge against unions. Of course, he was wrong about that. A host of other companies sprang up almost overnight as Detroit became the infamous Motor City. In the 1920s, Detroit was one of the world's foremost destinations.

My family certainly wasn't unique. The parents of Motown music founder Berry Gordy moved up from Georgia in 1922, drawn by the lure of the auto industry. Rep. John Conyers was born in Highland Park in 1929, the son of a labor leader in the auto industry. As a 5-year-old, Mayor Coleman Young moved north with his family from Alabama in 1923 for the same reason—good jobs. As a young man, Young cut his teeth in the labor unions that Ford doubted could spring up in such a diverse workforce. Like mine, Young's path led through the military. He was one of the famous Tuskegee Airmen. In the second half of the 20th century, Detroit's vibrant black community made its mark around the world. But, Henry Ford was right about one thing. Each racial and ethnic group wanted to retain its support network. Families carved out their own distinct neighborhoods of jam-packed homes, shops, houses of worship—and children spilling into the city's streets and schools. Tending to all those children were extended families and friends who embraced the familiar customs and values of home villages. Detroit neighborhoods often echoed traditions from the American South and from ethnic homelands all around the world.

So, I was raised by a village—and simply assumed that's how life should be. Everything went well as I attended Hamtramck schools, where my academic talents shone. My family's dream for me became more of a source of anxiety when I began my premed studies at Wayne University. I was an adequate student, not outstanding in my class. The truth was becoming painfully obvious to me: My family's high hopes for my future had no financial underpinning. Medical school tuition was far beyond my reach.

What I was to discover is that my family gave me far more than money. That was true for so many of us, even though we hardly appreciated that truth. At that time, no one had yet discovered the great black leaders who were just coming up in Detroit's neighborhoods. What we all knew instinctively was that life revolved around family. With that strength behind us, we could write the future.

My extended family was enormous and dispersed throughout the country. The Worthy clan was large, but my mother's Colbert family was enormous! My mother, Patsy Colbert Worthy, had 12 siblings and I grew up with 51 first cousins. Our generation raised hundreds of children. In addition to those huge numbers, family gatherings included an assortment of other down-home folks—members of the family by acclamation, if not a clear-cut connection on the genealogical chart.

When the Colberts called a family reunion, it was not uncommon for 500 to 1,000 men, women and children to show up. To the Colberts, especially the matriarchs and patriarchs of our clan, these gatherings represented an annual jubilee—a term from the Bible that described a celebration but also carried with it ancient associations of hope and justice. Anyone steeped in the black church understood the importance of such gatherings and the meaning of jubilee. These were times that fortified mind, body and spirit.

People came from near and far for these family reunions. They represented affluence and abject poverty; from free spirits to the deeply devout, from the illiterate to scholars in the highest echelons of education. Family pride neutralized all differences. All were welcome. For a few hours, everyone became a jewel of rare value. For as long as I can remember, searching for relatives we recognized among the crowds at these vast reunions was a time of tiptoe anticipation. When the first familiar face was sighted, the trials and terrors of the world were set aside for a little while.

The day before the reunion represented a traditional challenge. Someone had to spend the night on Detroit's Belle Isle to secure a desirable spot for the picnic. My cousin Jack Colbert always griped about it, but usually headed up this crucial effort. He knew that he had been selected because he was uniquely equipped—in fact and by reputation—to resist any challenge by others coveting the same corner of Belle Isle that he would select. He also knew that this was his unique contribution and that it was sincerely appreciated by everyone.

Food was laid out in communal fashion. Then the oldest man present would invoke God's blessing on "this food which we are about to receive for the nourishment of our bodies." The prayer was followed by expressions of concern that Aunt Ola might not have made her prized lemon and coconut cake; or fear that Aunt Veda's sweet potato pie would be consumed before one could get to the dessert end of the table. The diversity of food was as vast as the reunion—and certain dishes sparked tales that made stars of certain grand ladies in our family constellation. Over the years, for example, everyone knew the storied reputation of "Bertha's spaghetti" and vied for just a spoonful before it vanished. Each of the matriarchs had her own style. Some cooks humbly presented their dishes with little fanfare. Others took obvious pride. Still others clearly beamed at any praise for their dishes—and then feigned indifference. Surrounding the entire picnic site was an ambience of playful joshing that carried many relatives back to their Southern homes.

Picture-taking was an essential part of the festivities, although only a few were competent photographers. Each year, many showed up with new cameras that simply would not perform as they had so fondly hoped.

Some cameras were too complicated; others were so basic they could not compensate for variances in light, distance and movement at such an outdoor event. Often, photographers ran out of film or flashbulbs. None of that was cause for friction or frustration. What truly mattered was the great welling up of enthusiasm over posing for pictures that could be properly captured for posterity. Everyone wanted to be in the picture! The teasing and playful coaxing that accompanied the process—"Get in there a little closer, brother! I can't see you!"—ensured that everyone truly felt a part of the family.

That's why our games were regulated to allow easy entry into all activities without fear of rejection or embarrassment. The only requirement was enthusiasm. The chatter and jesting ultimately were all about encouragement and those loving expressions were more important than the games themselves. Hugs and gestures of approval made home runs unnecessary.

The joy of the day was never marred by overindulgence in alcohol. A few would exhibit signs of exuberance unattainable by consuming only fresh lemonade, but rarely was there physical evidence of the presence of alcohol. Drinking on these occasions was so controlled that I had grown considerably past the age of puberty before I could detect differences in behavior among those whom I later discovered to be imbibers on more than a casual basis. I could recall nothing in evidence at these gatherings that was not positive and uplifting.

Undergirding this remarkable tradition far more was the love and respect demonstrated for each other during the festivities themselves. These annual gatherings formed the visible body politic that assumed—that *knew* as bedrock faith—that each boy and girl would attain the best that he or she could dream. The reunions came with an unspoken corporate pledge that each man and woman was willing to sacrifice as required to help the next generation achieve those ends. These family conclaves built the support system that was to have a lasting impact on my life and that, when I became a husband and father myself, claimed my total allegiance.

In 1948, while I was studying at Wayne State University, I had the good fortune to meet Lillian Elizabeth Davis. The moment was a chance meeting among friends, but a connection was made almost instantly between two young people who had grown up with shared assumptions about family. The Davises were Georgia natives who migrated north while Lillian was in college. The family patriarch was Sam Davis, who was divorced and had the daunting task of raising three daughters. Lillian was his oldest. Like many black families in Detroit, Sam struggled to keep food on the family table. He rarely expressed emotion, but his quiet exterior seemed to mask a shrewd confidence that all would be well. I felt welcome in the Davis home, but there was always an air of suspense about this soft-spoken man. When I would visit, Sam hardly looked at me and usually would retire to the rear of their modest two-family flat on Detroit's East Side. Communication with Sam was a rarity.

Lillian clearly respected her father's guidance. She had stepped up to become more of a mother than a sister to her two younger siblings. Communication between family members seemed to be limited to Lillian's carefully orchestrated management of routine household affairs.

By the time I met Lillian, she already had graduated from Hudson High School in Macon, Georgia. Whenever she was faced with academic mysteries, she more than compensated through diligence and purposefulness. That's how she carved out her own pathway in life as well. She loved her family but would never lose her identity by sacrificing her personal goals. Lillian always managed to keep some distance between her family's needs and her personhood. She maintained an aura of tranquility but possessed a steely tenacity that would never accept defeat.

From the beginning, Lillian and I were attracted to each other partly because of our similarities. Both of us were tidy in thought and demeanor. Both of us were hard workers who would go to great lengths to make things turn out the way we thought they ought to be. Neither of us could rest until a task, once undertaken, was complete and in order. Even our differences were complementary. I appreciated Lillian's ability to immerse herself totally into any collective undertaking no matter how insignificant her part. I was not quite so selfless. In any group enterprise, I tended to gravitate quietly toward a position of leadership and was never content with monotony.

I was invited to attend the Lomax AME (African Methodist Episcopal) Zion Church, which was located a few blocks from the Davis residence, and I quickly realized that the church was the principal social outlet for the girls. On the other hand, Sam rarely went to church. For years, that has been the pattern in most of Detroit's historic black churches: The majority of attendees are women, although many men certainly do attend and many of them join the esteemed ranks as deacons, ushers and choir members. I found that going to church with Lillian was a good way to get to know her.

In her home, management of the Davises' meager resources was difficult. As a result, Lillian developed the habit of overcompensating for any extravagance by exercising prudence in near miserly proportions. Sam never objected to Lillian's unyielding insistence upon living within their means. Alma and Edith learned at a very early age that personal necessities were about all they could expect from the family coffer. Acquisitions aside from those essential to the routines of daily living had to be the product of personal initiative and resourcefulness.

Once Lillian and I found each other, there was never a thought of seeing someone else. Our exclusive commitment to each other was not verbalized. It was simply understood. My own resolute manner was apparently appreciated by Lillian. Our personalities dovetailed around our near-addiction to orderliness and an ironclad sense of living up to responsibilities we agreed to shoulder. Neither of us was extravagant. Whether looking through a mail-order catalog or looking over the shelves in stores, the convergence of our selections was uncanny. One could buy for the other with nearly complete confidence.

Of course, this turned out to be a fortunate background for the seemingly endless trials and travels of an Army wife.

There was one more value, or perhaps it was a talent, that sprang from the village by which I was raised. Competition permeated the fabric of family life for the Scott boys, my cousins, and I acquired a zeal for sports and an early awareness of their social benefits that was to serve me well in the future. There was no explaining my natural affinity for athletics, especially basketball and tennis, except that my experiences with the Scott family encouraged me to welcome new challenges and then to fully commit myself. While I never attended a basketball clinic nor took a formal tennis lesson, I had a knack for imitating the right moves and picking up techniques from more promising players. By the time I met Lillian, I was playing C-level tennis and had no difficulty picking up a game on the local high school courts.

I also learned a lot about family dynamics from my Aunt Bertha and Uncle Felton Scott, who had 10 children. I was their nephew, but in many respects, I became like an adopted son. Often, I would spend several days in their home with my cousins, totally assimilated into their household routine. Aunt Bertha personified the image of the strong black woman who kept her family together by force of personality—and she certainly did not exclude me from her strict disciplinary regimen! I very carefully avoided even the appearance of being at cross purposes with her. I had frequently witnessed instances of ill-conceived sibling misbehavior followed by Aunt Bertha's special form of corrective action. She took no prisoners! So, I decided that no temptation merited the risk of becoming the object of her wrath. In contrast, Uncle Felton was a gentle man who avoided Bertha's fury with a talent that her boys tried to emulate. He dearly loved his family and provided for them to the utmost of his ability. If asked to describe Uncle Felton, one would be compelled to exclaim with a certain reverence, "He was a good man!" There was only one moment in any day when the power in that home shifted from Aunt Bertha to Uncle Felton and it had to do with his public profession of faith. He would proudly tell anyone who asked that the Bible was his blueprint for life and Jesus was all-sufficient to his needs. Each night, Uncle Felton's prayer of praise, thanksgiving, and petition would reverberate throughout the small frame house with an authoritative ring. I was always astonished at that nightly transformation. From what I could see, Uncle Felton's prayers seemed totally inconsistent with his usual pattern of behavior—but I had to respect his commitment to that daily demonstration of spiritual authority. Aunt Bertha clearly welcomed it; and he happily complied.

No, my family did not have the financial resources that could turn the family dream of medical school into a reality for me. But the richness of the strong personalities and deep values that undergirded our village became the invaluable foundation that allowed me to face the many challenges that lay ahead.

West Point.

Henry Ossian Flipper.

3

The Road to West Point

*It is hereby declared to be the policy of the President that there shall
be equality of treatment and opportunity for all persons in the armed
services without regard to race, color, religion or national origin.*

Harry Truman, Executive Order 9981, July 26, 1948

*Pop was not an ideologue; he was a philosopher.
He did a lot of thinking on things where you
could make this country better, fairer.*

Rep. John Dingell Jr. describing Rep. John Dingell Sr.

Black young men did not dream of attending West Point when I was
growing up. That was a privileged preserve of white men whose families were among the elite or had somehow caught the attention of a U.S.
congressmen.

Anyone who took the time to research the history of black cadets
would have been scared away. I never so much as considered The Academy,
so I knew nothing about Henry Ossian Flipper (1856-1940), a former
slave from Georgia who was appointed to West Point after the Civil War
during Reconstruction. He suffered through years of abuse and relentless
isolation by his classmates. Cadets agreed that not a soul would talk to
him during his years at The Academy. Apparently, the other cadets never
violated that pact, even though at least one of the West Point instructors
stepped up to serve as his mentor and tutor for the tougher technical
courses. Somehow, Flipper persevered and became West Point's first black
graduate. He was assigned to the all-black "Buffalo Soldiers" in the West
and became the first black commander of Army troops in the field.

The second graduate, John Hanks Alexander (1864-1894), also survived a ruthless silencing from his peers. So did the third, Charles Young

(1864-1922), as well as the fourth, Benjamin O. Davis Jr. (1912-2002). Davis went on to become the first African-American 4-star general in the U.S. Air Force. When he was a cadet in the early 1930s, Davis endured a punishing isolation. He had no roommate, no friends and no one spoke to him. Recognizing that tragic history and Davis's heroic accomplishments in 2017, West Point named its newest barracks in Davis's honor—once again formally apologizing for turning such a promising cadet into "an invisible man" during his years at The Academy.

As I was attending Wayne State and struggling with my family's dream of becoming a physician, West Point had never entered my mind as a solution for my dilemma. I had never read the history of those early black cadets. In fact, no one had bothered to publish those histories! The door to West Point opened for me without any warning about what had happened in the past.

One day in 1946, I was walking through the front hall of Wayne State's Old Main building and noticed a young man in uniform looking at the student bulletin board. It was a uniform I recalled from photographs I had seen. Finally, I recognized that he was a West Point cadet. On an impulse, I introduced myself to Ed Wills, a one-time West Point cadet who had been discharged from The Academy. Ed seemed more than a little pleased that someone had noticed him and eagerly began a conversation that would reshape the course of my life. I would later reflect on this chance meeting and conclude that only Divine intervention could have so profoundly reconstructed my destiny.

Ed Wills was a tall, bronzed figure who almost always smiled as he spoke. His manner was disarming, and I was easily won over by his charm. At first, it did not occur to me to question why Ed continued to wear his uniform even after his severance from The Academy. Later I would surmise that Ed was simply clinging to the last vestige of his association with West Point.

Ed suggested that we have lunch together, during which I asked many questions about West Point. Each response seemed to kindle a new question followed by a new response that intensified the mystery and excitement surrounding these "Black Knights of the Hudson." When Ed perceived that I had more than just a casual interest in West Point, he suggested that I explore the possibility of obtaining an appointment.

I was visibly startled by the suggestion. This was a preposterous idea! Nevertheless, Ed was relentless. He made a simple and persuasive case: I was clearly interested; Ed's experience confirmed the possibility of admission for black cadets.

"The only thing you have to risk is the cost of a three-cent postage stamp," Ed concluded his case. "Why not try?"

After an exchange of phone numbers, Ed departed, and I sat for a long time contemplating my future. The prospects of my acceptance into medical school and absorbing the associated costs were zero—about the same long-shot odds as attending West Point. I wondered if I should waste the time of writing a letter. However, Ed's reasoning seemed unimpeachable. There really was nothing to lose but a three-cent stamp. So, I quickly composed a letter on the back of a paper place mat, which I later transposed onto university stationery before mailing it to Rep. John Dingell Sr., Democrat from Michigan's 15th congressional district in western Detroit.

I decided that the whole idea was so farfetched that I would tell no one and began to condition myself to avoid the disappointment of rejection—if indeed there would be any response at all.

There was so much I did not know about this doorway ahead of me. I certainly did not know the long history of silenced black cadets. I also was unaware of the complex, decade-long struggle over racial barriers in the U.S. armed forces. In 1941, President Roosevelt had signed Executive Order 8802, which was the first federal action to promote racial equality by prohibiting discrimination in defense industries. This was a pragmatic step by the president. Our nation needed to take a huge leap onto a full-scale war footing and all able-bodied workers should be employed, Roosevelt reasoned. His order was a historic milestone—but, by the end of the war, Jim Crow restrictions remained throughout the armed forces. For example, black recruits had to wait years for any shot at specialized training opportunities that were routinely available to promising white recruits. Complex racial barriers ran throughout all branches of the service. In 1947, civil rights leader A. Philip Randolph zeroed in on these disparities, forming the Committee Against Jim Crow in Military Service. President Truman regarded these ideas as simply common sense and a matter of basic fairness. By the summer of 1948, he signed Executive Order 8891, calling for the end to racial discrimination in the armed forces.

Although major U.S. newspapers covered this milestone with skepticism that anything would change in the military, the famous African-American newspaper *The Chicago Defender* published a banner front-page headline: **President Truman Wipes Out Segregation in Armed Forces.**

Of course, my encounter with Ed Wills and my three-cent-stamped letter all took place in 1946, before Randolph started his effort and two years before Truman's order. But, in that era right after the war, I wasn't alone in suddenly waking up to the possibility of an appointment to West Point. Around the time I sent in my application, a young man from St. Louis had applied, and had been accepted in 1947. Eventually, we were at The Academy together. He was Roscoe Robinson Jr., who, just like me, had started college in his home city and had become aware of new possibilities at West Point. Robinson started at The Academy before I did and, much later, went on to become the first 4-star general in the U.S. Army.

America certainly had not shed its ugly Jim Crow laws and traditions overnight. This was still decades before the Civil Rights Act of 1964. One of the leading post-war figures in Michigan who had decided that basic injustices had to be corrected in our American culture was Rep. John Dingell Sr. In 1894, he was born John Dzieglewicz, the son of Polish immigrants who came to Detroit in the hope of finding work—just like my family, who had arrived from the South. Along with industrial jobs came the reality that working families had to have basic legal protections. Dzieglewicz decided to run for office. First, he changed his surname to the more memorable "Dingell," which produced the slogan "Ring in with Dingell!" With that campaign, he won a seat in Congress in 1933. After World War II, Congressman Dingell pushed for a broad agenda of what he described as justice issues for all American workers, including breaking down racial barriers. He even campaigned for national health insurance, back when such an idea seemed utopian. He would serve until his death in 1955, when his son John Dingell Jr. won that seat in a special election and would become the longest-serving congressman in U.S. history.

I had no grand vision of this historic transformation. When I sent in my letter, some of these events had already unfolded—some had not yet occurred. I knew nothing about all of these key players moving across the grand chessboard of American life. It wasn't my own brilliance that pushed me toward that historic doorway. I believe it was Providence. For weeks, after mailing off my letter, I simply went on with my studies, played tennis, spent time with Lillian and had almost forgotten about what I was about to unleash.

Then, a congressionally franked letter arrived in our mailbox. My mother intercepted the letter and anxiously pondered what might be inside the sealed envelope while she waited for me to get home. Mom always tended to take a morbid view of the unknown. It would never occur to her that a letter with such imposing markings could bear good news. She placed the letter against the centerpiece on the kitchen table and waited.

When I got home, I immediately went to the kitchen, as I always did, and there sat Mom, strategically positioned so that she could see my face as I opened the letter.

"Do you know anything about this?" she asked, dramatically drawing my attention to that fateful envelope.

My first reaction was one of disappointment. I had not mentioned my application to anyone and now I would have to take time to explain the history behind this letter, which I assumed was a rejection. I was tired after a long day and just wanted to go to bed. I have to admit that I must have seemed rude, because I did not answer her at first.

I simply picked up the letter and began to examine it. The envelope did, indeed, look official. I carefully released the flap of the envelope, as if a single tear would desecrate its contents. Even as I peered inside, I suddenly felt excitement welling up inside. I dared to wonder: *In this moment, could my life change?* Unexpected and unlikely as it was, that envelope *was* a pivotal moment in my life.

The letter was brief and almost too positive to be believed. I was totally unprepared for the casual and reassuring tone of the note, which suggested a more than even chance that I could receive one of the most coveted prizes available to any young man in America. The letter from Congressman Dingell requested additional information and asked for transcripts of my grades and directed contact with civic leaders.

I did not know what to say. I managed to utter the words: "Here, Mama, read it for yourself."

Mom was puzzled by what she saw. She had heard about West Point but didn't know that it was the home of the United States Military Academy. She had seen a newsreel in which West Point cadets were on parade and had decided that it must be a special place. She had no concept of its academic tradition or its association with the military. It was out there someplace in the "for whites only" world, like Hollywood or major league baseball.

It was not that Mom was ignorant of world news. Quite the contrary, she was probably the most literate of the Colbert clan. As a young adult, she had been the school mistress for the only school available to blacks in Crawford County, Georgia. She loved reading but had been limited to a haphazard library of dog-eared volumes considered appropriate for smart "nigras." In later life, she had attempted to make up for years of literary deprivation through voracious reading. But, West Point? That certainly had not been on her reading list.

West Point was simply beyond the dreams of black families. At that point, few people aside from The Academy's archivists knew anything about those pioneering black cadets. This was two years before African-American newspapers and magazines would carry news of Truman's dramatic decree from the White House. This was a moment when our entire nation was about to begin pivoting on its racial axis, but that awareness today comes only in hindsight. On the day that letter landed on our kitchen table, Mom had no way of knowing that our household was about to play a part in a new national drama.

Mom sat there silently. She simply waited for me to explain.

So, as tired as I was after a long day, the whole story began to spill out of me. I told her about the bulletin board and Ed Wills—and my fear that medical school was out of reach. I told her about my letter and the three-cent stamp.

I fully expected some expression of deep disappointment over my willingness to abandon my medical career. I was also beginning to anticipate a flood of objections from relatives who had collectively decided that I would become the family doctor.

Much to my amazement, Mom said nothing about my medical career. Instead, she immediately began musing over prospects for the two references requested in Congressman Dingell's letter.

Now that her fears had subsided, Mom surprised me by admitting that this letter might be the answer to her prayers. That's when I realized that I was not alone in understanding that medical school was an impossible dream. Mom had been cherishing that dream as fondly as anyone, but Mom knew the hard truth. For two years, she had been separated from Dad after their rocky marriage had become untenable. She was virtually a single parent. Mom had been praying about my future perhaps harder than anyone else in my life. Now I could see her carefully weighing this news. Could this letter be the deliverance from the yoke of unrealistic family expectations for my career—a dilemma that she had offered up in prayer so many times?

I understood the situation she faced every day, trying to make ends meet. To compensate for my father's shortcomings by her standards, Mom had seized every opportunity to farm me out to selected male members of the extended family to assure my exposure to "proper" male role models. In keeping with that approach to family life, Mom responded to the letter by listing potential male mentors in the extended family who we could consult for advice on how to best respond. In this instance, I eliminated the need for any family intervention by informing Mom that I would contact Roy Morton the next day. Roy Morton was one of the best-known blacks on Detroit's northwest side at that time. I knew Roy's two daughters on a casual basis and hoped that they would boost my appeal to their father. I was right in my estimation of how that connection could be made.

After reading the letter, Roy assured me that he would be delighted to do what he could. He further volunteered to deliver the second endorsement requested by Congressman Dingell. Nothing that I had attempted in the past had been this easy. Everything seemed to be falling into place.

I made the necessary arrangements to provide the transcript of my grades and Roy Morton's response was swift and convincing. His special relationship with Congressman Dingell negated the need for a second reference. His good word on my behalf was sufficient.

Arranging for the release of transcripts was not without complications. I discovered that some Wayne State officials were skeptical about the validity of the request. A "colored" student asking for transcripts to be sent to a congressman pursuant to admission to West Point was unprecedented at the university.

Mom already had taken it upon herself to activate the Colbert grapevine. Within 48 hours, all branches had been notified. There was no formalized communications system; everyone seemed to intuitively know whom to call with a minimum of redundancy. I was relieved to learn that Mom had received a nearly unanimous vote of support for this change in the family's agenda. Only a handful of diehards expressed disappointment.

The encounter with Ed Wills in 1946 and the affirmation by Congressman Dingell of my quest for a West Point appointment were the beginning of a prolonged process before fruition. There were still admissibility obstacles to be overcome before all the dots could be connected for acceptance to The Academy. What impresses me now, as I look back on that remarkable process, is that Congressman Dingell never gave up on me. He saw the larger drama that was unfolding nationwide. He knew about Randolph's efforts against Jim Crow barriers in the armed forces. He supported Truman's executive order. The drama unfolded, step by step, and the doors of West Point finally opened to me on July 1, 1949.

Our progress as cadets was followed by the NAACP, including coverage
in the national magazine, The Crisis, founded by W.E.B. DuBois in
1910. In the May 1950 issue, this full-page photograph appeared. The
reproduction was not ideal, but we were certainly proud to appear in
that magazine. The original caption, written in the style of that era,
said: "The Six Negro Cadets attending the U.S. Military Academy at
West Point are shown standing on the steps off of Washington Hall.
First row L to R: Cadets Bernard C. Hughes, Washington, D.C.;
Gerald W. Corprew, Bronx, NY; Clifford Worthy, Detroit, Mich.;
and Norman J. Brown, Philadelphia, Pa.; Back row L to R: Cadets
James R. Young, Brooklyn, NY; and Roscoe Robinson, Jr., St. Louis,
Mo." Of this group of pioneers, Robinson rose furthest in the ranks,
becoming the first African-American 4-star general in the U.S. Army.

Cadets starting senior year are allowed to wear a class ring, which we would wear with the inscription facing toward us until we graduated. Lillian came to West Point for that milestone, marked by a formal dance called the Ring Hop. After graduation, the ring is turned so that anyone we meet can see the inscription.

At a West Point awards ceremony, I wore my summer
parade uniform, complete with the sword at my side.

Before West Point, I had never played squash. With the expert training of our Coach Leif Nordlie, I became the captain of the squash team.

Our tennis team was fortunate to play under Coach Nordlie, who was one of the most successful coaches in the history of Army's tennis teams.

4

The West Point Years

Whatever enables us to go to war—secures our peace.

Thomas Jefferson, who supported West Point's creation in 1802

Duty. Honor. Country.

West Point's motto

The welcome to West Point was anything but hospitable. Having spent most of my life in a slower-paced community where I was able to successfully navigate with modest exertions of energy—I was not prepared for the highly charged challenges of West Point.

Years later, many West Point graduates look back nostalgically on the gut-wrenching terror of their first contact with the Long Gray Line, The Academy's way of referring to the unbroken line of graduates and cadets that passed through its halls. Trauma was tradition. For weeks, newcomers were subjected to what was known as Beast Barracks, a time-tested process of turning civilians into cadets. This heavy-duty introduction to the traditions and regimens of West Point was boot camp—and more. The effort was a carefully orchestrated attempt to convince the heartiest new candidate that he no longer controlled his own life. The conductors of this process were collectively called the Beast Detail, seniors known as first classmen at The Academy.

Looking at the process as a young man, fresh off a train from Michigan and trying to make my way up the hill to The Academy, this was a full-force ordeal. The Beast Detail seemed all knowing and all powerful. They swooped in from the moment we disembarked and started up the hill. They knew just how to engender the right mix of fear, mystery and awe.

We all dreaded hearing one of their barked commands. We had to obey.

For me, there was no question of failure. I could not turn back. I had to persevere. At least, by 1949, black cadets were no longer subject to years of silencing.

Coming off those trains with me that year were young men, aged 17 to 21, who were funneled into The Academy from every socio-economic stratum, ethnicity, creed and race. Like me, they were forced to shed their individual identities and backgrounds. To survive, they had to adopt a whole new culture that was exclusively West Point. Whether we came from high or low status, wealth or poverty, we all were cast off whatever perch or pinnacle we had previously enjoyed. Now, we were merely plebes. We might have arrived as our proud parents' sons, but we walked into The Academy as the property of West Point. As I stepped through those doors, I remember how terrified and yet proud I was that I had a chance to become a part of all this. I belonged here. No one was going to oust me. I was going to stay.

If I thought my family's dream of medical school had hung heavy on my shoulders—that was nothing compared to the steel regimen that now surrounded me at every turn. We began with orderly clothing distribution, room assignments, haircuts, and the issuing of a rifle and bayonet. We were immersed in regimental, battalion, company, platoon and squad orientations. We tried to follow our first close-order drill.

Every phase of daily life was regimented, including what was known as Shower Formation, when we had to line up and each one of us had to report to our squad leader:

"Sir! New Cadet Worthy reports that I have brushed my teeth, have my soap dish and had my last bowel movement at 0600 hours. Sir!"

Some guys simply could not function under such intense scrutiny and encountered problems right away. I managed to comply with these intrusive rules and the squad leader would accept my report—and then allow me exactly 30 seconds to shower.

Our days were packed with instruction on shoe-shining, clothing display, weapons disassembly and cleaning, polishing of brass on our uniforms, bed-making, physical training, mess hall protocol—and knowledge of a whole long list of academy trivia commonly referred to as Plebe Poop. Those were just some of the "character enhancements" that comprised West Point's special brand of basic training.

Everything we did was overlaid with a continuous indoctrination in the West Point Honor Code: "A cadet will not lie, cheat, steal or tolerate those who do."

No facet of human behavior touching on the makeup of an officer and a gentleman was omitted from the Beast Barracks agenda. Every minute of July and August was filled with such diverse activities as bayonet drills and marches in full combat gear—to the subtleties of proper place settings in the dining room. Our cadet hostess, Miss Barth, conducted our etiquette training, which included instruction in ballroom dancing.

Indeed, the mission of the Beast Detail was to transform approximately 800 Dumb Johns into neophyte members of the Long Grey Line, contingent upon their demonstration of rudimentary potential to become officers and gentlemen. Approximately 50 failed to reach that first plateau and were sent home.

Early in September, plebes were assigned to companies according to their height. This assured uniformity in ranks during parades. It also minimized the visual distraction of bodies seeming to bob along due to a mix of long and short strides. Only in the case of the black cadets was there an exception to this rule. All black cadets in each class were required to room together regardless of height. Bernard Hughes was a full four inches shorter than Gerry Corprew and I—the only other blacks in the plebe class. During drill and parades, Bernard would be posted to an interior position in the ranks and forced to develop an exaggerated gait in order to keep in step. The combination of being the youngest of the three blacks and being the company runt severely tested Bernard's resolve to beat the plebe system.

September, the end of Beast Barracks, could not come soon enough for Bernard. He had been an academic All-American at Dunbar High School in Washington, D.C. The Hughes family had built a tradition of academic excellence at Dunbar and Bernard was determined to prove that he could compete with the best. Now, West Point had become Bernard's comeuppance. Trivial events designed to test the resiliency of plebes became emotional disasters for him. He had been humiliated to the point of tears on several occasions and only a strong sense of pride had kept him from throwing in the towel.

In contrast, Gerry Corprew was a free spirit. He delighted in bucking the system but knew when to take on a posture of conformance when it was in his best interest to do so. He had little patience with Bernard's outbursts of frustration. He knew that his brinksmanship tactics in defiance of the plebe system intensified Bernard's already exaggerated sense of doom. Gerry was from the Bronx and typically exhibited a hard-core New Yorker's penchant for survival. He had attended New York University and bragged that his courses had been so demanding that he could not afford the luxury of a lunch break. He had been "forced" to eat his lunch in the men's room while responding to the urgings of nature. Even after four years had passed, I could never be sure which of Gerry's offbeat remarks were for real and which were for effect.

Like Bernard, Gerry was an intellectual heavyweight. For Bernard, studying was a labor of love. For Gerry, it was a necessary evil in which one should never overindulge nor take too seriously. Both had distinguished themselves as scholars. Bernard was destined for higher academic standing because he constantly reached for the stars, but Gerry was content to tease the establishment. Both easily outdistanced me in the scientific disciplines that constituted the heart of the West Point curriculum.

The academic system was designed to promote diligence as well as excellence on the part of every cadet. No cadet, no matter how gifted, could take the risk of deferring daily study in favor of the more conventional pattern of procrastination followed by cramming for a prescheduled examination. There were daily study assignments preliminary to some form of daily measurement of proficiency attained in each given area. These evaluations could take the form of quizzes, verbal responses to an instructor's questions or any other technique deemed appropriate by the professor. Typical in math and science classes were blackboard drills.

"Take boards!" was an almost daily order that required us to shoot to our feet, move immediately to our specific areas of the classroom's blackboards and take up chalk to chart our solutions to whatever problem was assigned.

As the professor moved around the room, each of us had to be prepared to give a detailed explanation of our solution, to answer challenges to our work and to maintain a formal and respectful tone in every word that came from our mouths.

The problem quickly became obvious: We had to fulfill every requirement because we might be tested at any moment—yet there was never
enough time to meet all the requirements. That was part of the West Point
process as well. Learning to budget our time was as much a test of a
cadet's resourcefulness as his ability to complete assignments.

Initially, cadets were alphabetically placed into classroom sections
that rarely consisted of more than 12 members. After a specified period
of time, cadets were re-sectioned based upon performance. Subsequent
re-sectioning would take place on a monthly basis, enabling unlimited
upward—or downward—mobility depending upon individual persever-
ance and enlightenment. The maximum achievable grade was 3.0. All
of us dreaded the penalties accruing to those falling below a minimum
grade point average of 2.0—including potential dismissal. This system
had many sticks and carrots. Beyond the stick of a possible ouster, there
also were substantive carrots offered to those who earned places in the
higher sections. Upper-section cadets were afforded greater opportunity
for in-depth exploration with the professors. They could soar far beyond
the core curriculum that was taught to the "goat" sections.

When describing West Point culture in that era, however, one must
hasten to add that the "goats" did not necessarily suffer from classmates'
derision. West Point culture and status was far more complex than that.
In fact, there was more than a century of goat lore behind us by the time
I arrived at The Academy—so many stories that they have literally filled
other history books. For example, before the annual Army-Navy football
game, there was a West Point-only football game between a team made
up of goats and one made up of their academic superiors. If the goats
won, that year's West Point team likely was tougher and was more likely
to beat Navy. Through such avenues, the goats acquired their own forms
of gutsy respect. Today, West Point's most famous goat was Gen. George
Armstrong Custer, last in the class of 1861—just in time to become a hero
in the Civil War and later to meet tragedy in the West.

My roommates and I became painfully aware of all these dangers, challenges and opportunities that lay ahead of us at The Academy. Driven by an
obsession to perpetuate the Hughes family tradition of scholastic prowess,
Bernard excelled across the board. Gerry lacked Bernard's intensity and
commitment but nearly matched his record of academic achievement. I

excelled in my foreign language classes and in the humanities, but at times flirted with disaster in the engineering sciences.

I wound up excelling in another unexpected area of academy life. Our academic buildings and library were clustered near the Corps Squad tennis courts. Passing by one day, I observed plebe tennis team prospects going through proficiency drills. As I watched the less-than-spectacular play, I decided to try out. Unknowing, I had made a decision of far-reaching consequences that nearly rivaled the opportunity I encountered that day I stumbled into Ed Wills at Wayne State.

I made the team by a comfortable margin and my selection as the first black to play Corps Squad tennis broke new and somewhat hallowed ground. I became a minor celebrity and began to enjoy the perks reserved for plebe athletes. These included "recognition," which meant that some of the typical harassment of plebes was set aside in my case. I now also enjoyed a special menu reserved for West Point athletes. Our tennis schedule eventually carried me into contact with prestigious Ivy League schools—a highly coveted privilege denied the vast majority of plebes, who were destined to spend the entire first year within the confines of West Point. Most importantly, Corps Squad membership provided an additional channel to demonstrate leadership abilities so important to the academy's ranking of each cadet's military aptitude.

Through the Corps Squad, I also met a first classman who introduced me to a new dimension of the West Point experience. The cadet was a boxer and a deeply committed Christian. He was a soft-spoken South Dakotan who exuded confidence. I had never met anyone who seemed less intimidated by all the tradition and trappings of West Point. He invited me to attend a daily devotional service held at the chaplain's office each morning. Cadets who desired to be a part of this fellowship were permitted to leave the mess hall before the conclusion of breakfast. The devotions were conducted by cadets on a rotating basis and consisted of the singing of hymns, followed by a Scripture reading and personal testimonies. It was a time of refreshing, sharing and spiritual rejuvenation. Picture an assembly of young men from a variety of ethnic groups, economic and social strata, political persuasions and cultural inclinations putting aside the veneer of West Point for a brief period each day to celebrate the sustaining power and love of Jesus Christ. There was no need for sham or pretense here.

By the world's standards, all were men of the highest caliber who had demonstrated potential for greatness, yet each had without coercion surrendered his own will to the sovereignty of the triune God. They were not foxhole Christians turning to God out of fear or desperation. Theirs was a simple recognition that they were *who* they were and *where* they were by God's grace and shared a common desire to continually offer up praise and thanksgiving.

In January 1950, I became a daily participant in the after-breakfast devotionals. I eagerly embraced this fellowship and discovered a whole new spiritual awareness of the "peace which passes understanding."

Wrapped up in this new commitment to Christ and new confidence in my place at The Academy, I crossed a crucial line of demarcation in my entire attitude toward life at West Point. I managed to set aside my fears and uncertainties and move forward with a confidence that I can only describe as blessed assurance. I was still dazzled by West Point, but no longer intimidated. My spirit had spiraled to a takeoff point that vectored me toward my destined rendezvous with the Long Grey Line. My spiritual mentor in this part of my journey was Pete Monfore, one of 28 members of the class of 1950 who "gave the last full measure of their devotion" while fighting in the Korean conflict shortly after graduation. I will never forget Pete's positive impact on my life.

The ensuing three-and-a-half years leading up to graduation overflowed with challenges and achievements. Based upon appraisals by peers, upperclassmen and tactical officers, I was appointed Cadet Corporal—a rank awarded to second classmen (juniors) demonstrating the highest military aptitude. I was told that was a first-ever honor for any black cadet. I was also voted captain of the squash team during my first-class year— another first—despite the fact that I had never played the sport before entering West Point.

Back in 1950, Lillian Davis and I had become engaged during her first visit to West Point. She had graduated from Wayne State in 1949—the month after I entered The Academy. When she visited, I had arranged for her to stay at The Academy's Thayer Hotel, located just inside the main gate. It was a delightful old inn named after the father of West Point, Sylvanus Thayer. It was a perfect extension of the West Point experience and stood as if hewn from the same granite and fashioned by the same architect as West Point's historic quadrangles and sally ports.

To Lillian, everything about West Point suggested strength and stability. Even cadet frivolity exuded a kind of ordered reaction to an unwavering history. It was as if West Point generated its own magnetic field. The long grey lines of flux were irresistibly drawn into West Point's black, gold and grey heart—never to escape. West Point was bound by its own peculiar and immutable law of continuity. It was not that nothing ever changed at West Point. On the contrary, substantive change occurred more rapidly at West Point than at other major universities because of the frequent turnover of faculty and administrators. With the exception of academic department heads, chaplains, coaches and a few civilian instructors, West Point's complement of staff and faculty, including the superintendent, usually departed after a three-year tour of duty. In such an environment, new ideas were welcomed as long as they did not threaten the West Point continuum.

Standing on the steps of the Cadet Chapel that appeared to be chiseled out of the rock on which it stood, Lillian would gaze down upon the West Point Plain, which was skirted by noble monuments of granite and stone with all of their spectacular symmetry and historical linkages. Her head would spin with grand notions that her children would spring forth from the seeds that had fallen into the good soil that was West Point. Nothing would prevail against them. They would be lovely children, nurtured by quality parents who would hold to the highest standards of the family ethic.

June Week, 1953—the week preceding graduation—marked the end of my four years at West Point and the beginning of a new life for Lillian and me. It was a festive week filled with athletic contests, dances, parades, the Superintendent's Reception, and other traditional soirees, culminating in graduation exercises.

Graduation Parade was one of the premier events of the week. It was the only parade that no one wanted to miss. A supercharged excitement permeated the barracks as cadets of all classes checked their uniforms and equipment prior to assembly in the company areas. Upperclassmen braced smirking plebes for the last time. Every plebe basked in the knowledge that his participation in the parade meant that he had crossed the burning sands to reach another milestone and was now ready to move up the next rung on the ladder of the Long Grey Line. For the plebe, the "recognition" that would follow could be likened to the elation of winning Olympic Gold. After a final Pass in Review, the Corps would be dismissed. Immediately following the dismissal, all plebes would form a line by company and each upperclassman would extend his hand in an emotionally charged gesture of acceptance that confirmed full standing in the Corps of Cadets! Recognition removed all barriers and a oneness of purpose and spirit was experienced that perhaps would never again be equaled. To say that this was pretty heady stuff for a young black boy from the heart of Detroit's inner city was a colossal understatement.

All of the June Week activities were precursory to graduation. Hollywood could not have improved upon the imagery of that occasion. Five hundred and twelve cadets neatly arrayed in their full-dress grey over white uniforms strategically positioned in the Field House listened to the challenges and admonitions of General Matthew Ridgeway. This was followed by each cadet marching up the ramp in academic rank order to smartly salute and receive his diploma. Finally, the customary cheer for the class goat was followed by the tossing of white hats into the air, which represented the last traditional act of departing cadets.

The crowning event of the most significant week of my life would take place the next day. Our wedding was scheduled for 10 a.m. on Wednesday, June 3, 1953, at the Cadet Chapel. It would be one of 20 weddings scheduled for that day. To be married at West Point was the dream of a lifetime for Lillian. She could not contain the excitement she felt as she shared her plans with Sam, Alma and Edith, as well as her close friends. The logistical challenges that came with marriage at West Point were of little concern to her. She would find a way, no matter the economics or other constraints, to get the wedding party to the appointed place. I was not privy to Lillian's detailed planning. For me, it all just seemed to fall in place. I was not aware of all of Lillian's efforts to coordinate travel for both families, assure acquisition of proper attire by all involved, complete all required documentation and the myriad of other items incidental to the wedding. My only task was to assemble the saber bearers to form the arch under which Lillian and I would pass as we departed the chapel.

Considering the expenses and distance involved, there was excellent representation by both families. The Detroit contingent consisted of Sam, Alma, Edith and Lillian's bridesmaid, Grace King, on the Davis side; and Patsy and a host of Colberts, Scotts, and their spouses and friends. Bernard, J.O. Dritt, Bob Albert and Drew Dowling made up the cadet participants in the wedding. My cousin Dwight Scott was the best man. The Rev. Frank Pulley, the cadet chaplain, officiated using the traditional Episcopal order of service.

Lillian could not have been more pleased. To her, the combination of military academy efficiency and Episcopalian pomp and structure presaged a marriage as rock solid as West Point itself. Chaplain Pulley's "man and wife" pronouncement sealed the union with the same ring of finality as the clanging of the Thayer gate at the entrance to West Point.

The setting was perfect in every respect. Lillian and I emerged from the chapel onto a parapet overlooking the entire panorama of The Academy converging onto the breathtaking banks of the Hudson River. Against this backdrop, pictures were composed, taking full advantage of that scenery with allowance—followed by a gentle nudge off the premises to prepare for the next ceremony in that long day of weddings. It was all carefully orchestrated to assure a memorable experience despite the clockwork scheduling of the facilities.

After the ceremony, Lillian and I immediately finished packing our belongings into our new 1953 Ford and left family and friends to fend for themselves, assisted by Lillian's prearranged plans for their return to Detroit. Lillian and I were particularly proud of that new Ford. We had jointly saved for three years in order to pay cash for a car upon my graduation. We decided upon a Ford because a Newburgh, New York dealer offered the car nearly at manufacturer's cost, a total of $1,714, to first classmen.

As we departed West Point, all I could think of was Paul's second letter to the Corinthians and his lines, "The old things have passed away; behold, all things have become new."

As Lillian and I eased onto the highway toward Detroit, the ominous weight of such a brand new horizon began to settle on my shoulders. My spirit soared, but then I also began to ponder all the uncertainties ahead of us.

I glanced to my right at Lillian. She was staring straight ahead, looking pensively down the road, but she sensed my need for reassurance. Lillian moved closer to me and began caressing the back of my neck.

Then, nothing else mattered.

We were driving along the old Highway 17 to connect through Virginia with routes back to Michigan. It was the perfect road for two newlyweds who had been sheltered from the rigors and hubbub of interstate commerce. A quiet, undulating, mostly two-lane road punctuated by sleepy intersections and small towns, it allowed Lillian and I to focus on more important things, like each other. It was the first time that we had spent five hours together without a third party to chaperone.

Little was verbalized. Much was conveyed between us. A gesture, a nod or an affirmative touch communicated more than a thousand well-chosen words.

Around 6 p.m., we began searching for lodging. It was 1953 and we were apprehensive about the reception that we might receive when requesting accommodations. I had prayed to myself that our wedding night would not be spoiled by a racially motivated rebuff. We both decided upon a small but well-kept motel that had evidence of just a few patrons. We were greatly relieved by the warmth of the desk clerk, who seemed to be unconcerned about the color of our skin.

After checking in, we went immediately to the dining room, where we were pleased to note that there were only two other tables being served and none of the customers seemed to take special note of us. The waitress was genuinely friendly. Lillian and I detected none of the insolence often expressed by those who somehow feel violated when forced to serve guests of another race. Thirty-four years later, I would find a copy of the dinner menu and the paid receipt amongst Lillian's keepsakes.

After a night of discovery and fulfillment, Lillian and I were bound for whatever Providence placed ahead of us.

Lillian in 1951.

On our wedding day, we processed from the church
under raised sabers, held by four of my friends.

5

Americans in Motion

Into each life, some rain must fall.

The Ink Spots, 1944

Have I not commanded you?
Be strong and courageous.
Do not be afraid; do not be discouraged, for the Lord
your God will be with you wherever you go.

Joshua 1:9

Americans were on the move in the early 1950s. Kemmons Wilson built his first Holiday Inn in Memphis in 1952 and dreamed of one day having comfortable affordable little inns coast to coast. Ray Kroc met the McDonald brothers in 1954 and soon began dreaming of a nationwide chain of simple family restaurants. Disneyland opened in 1955. President Eisenhower came into office in 1953, knowing that he had to kickstart the American system of cross-country roads and in 1956 signed the National Interstate and Defense Highways Act.

Lillian and I were on the move, too. Of course, that was long before corporate visionaries and our national leaders came to terms with what it meant to provide equal access—or even safe passage—to all of the millions of families traveling our highways. The Supreme Court issued its historic *Brown v. Board of Education* ruling in 1954, Emmett Till was murdered in 1955 and that same year Rosa Parks refused to give up her seat on a bus.

When Lillian and I headed out for Detroit in 1953, America was a patchwork quilt of communities, some welcoming people of color as a natural part of American hospitality—and some still dangerously hostile. Our journey back to Detroit was uneventful. Five days following our wedding at West Point, 120 friends and family were invited to a reception in Detroit. I readily consented to wear my brand-new second lieutenant's uniform. It was also an opportunity to show off my prized blue sapphire class ring with the wedding band designed to fit the curvature of the ring. It was truly a gala affair. Lillian's best friend, Grace King, had planned well.

I had never seen Lillian so animated as she was that evening. A classic low-key personality, Lillian was more vivacious than I had ever witnessed before.

Grace teased her: "Is this the Lillian I know?"

Most of the faces were new to me but all were friendly and eagerly searching for clues to the chemistry that brought Lillian and me together. Many expressed real or feigned envy at the prospect of excitement and adventure that Army life would bring. Some tried to veil their pity for Lillian, who they perceived as facing a spartan existence or, at best, a life just above the subsistence level.

Lillian again surprised me by spontaneously announcing to all our guests that we would be leaving on the following Monday for a 10-day honeymoon trip to Martha's Vineyard. How could we possibly afford that? Back when I entered West Point, the president of a Detroit trade association for African-Americans had donated the $300 fee for clothing that was required for new West Point cadets. Now, that same business-man made reservations for us at a lodge on the island. Our destination was no secret, but I was astonished by Lillian's uncharacteristically public announcement. These were the first signs of Lillian's breakout from her introverted past.

Martha's Vineyard, indeed the whole New England scene, was a revelation to Lillian and me. We were unprepared for the power and grandeur of land meeting sea around the entire Cape Cod area. Both of us were awestruck by the majesty of the ocean with its relentless wind and waves—rising and falling as if testing the resolve of the entire continent. While on the island, we became beach bums, fishermen, shell-seekers and moon-bathers. We built sand castles, discerned the stars and faced the wind. Never again would we be as unencumbered as we were those few precious days.

Except for the owner, we were the only tenants in the lodge at that time. All of the facilities were at our disposal at any time and the owner was grateful for our company. We feasted on homemade clam chowder, several species of fish that were new to us and learned to love the ambience of sea and shore. The owner, a widow who lived alone, seemed to sense when her presence was no longer adding value to any occasion and would disappear into the woodwork at the appropriate time.

The end of the Martha's Vineyard chapter in our lives came much too quickly for Lillian. There had not been a single downside to the entire experience. As we rode the ferry back to the mainland en route to Detroit again, Lillian stared at the Vineyard as if indelibly fixing its image into her memory to be recalled when needed to soothe the troubled waters ahead.

The road to Fort Sill, Oklahoma, was not as hospitable as the highways we had traveled so far. At that time, as an African-American couple traveling cross-country, we carefully packed enough food to last for our entire two-day journey. This time, we were traveling south. We did not even consider stopping at local businesses before reaching St. Louis, Missouri. We braced ourselves against the intensely debilitating summer heat from the start of our trip, but we were not prepared for the humidity as we reached the outskirts of the city.

The only known "colored" hotel in St. Louis was a disaster. The lobby was uninhabited except for a sleepy and ill-tempered desk clerk who obviously resented being disturbed. The hotel register consisted of a single sheet of lined paper with no heading or other entries. The towels that the clerk tossed onto the counter told the tale: so stale and dingy that we wondered if they had even been washed between patrons. The elevators were inoperative, forcing us to negotiate oppressively hot and dimly lit stairs enclosed by crumbling walls and poorly maintained handrails.

Finally, we reached our floor, stepped out of the stairwell into our hallway—and Lillian was sure she saw movement! Something scurried away from our doorway and disappeared into the shadows.

"No way!" That was Lillian's verdict.

We returned to the front desk and asked about other accommodations. Our rejection of the room was obviously not unexpected by the clerk, who almost cheerfully advised us to try a newly opened colored motel. We were curious, to say the least. This was 1953, years before cross-country travelers could expect to find standardized motor inns near every major city. Kemmons Wilson didn't even think of calling his little business

"Holiday Inn of America" until 1957. So, when we wheeled into this motel parking lot, Lillian remained in the car while I checked on this new place. What I discovered was a well-lit, air-conditioned lobby. I turned back and motioned Lillian to join me.

I was already at the desk, talking to the owner, who seemed delighted at our patronage. Lillian came through the door and was visibly relieved! While far from luxurious, this business was clean and inviting. The owner clearly was striving to run a first-class operation. His employees were still a bit awkward, we discovered. Like the owner, they were just learning how to run such a business. But they politely ushered us to our room. Lillian expressed her approval by executing a gleeful pirouette followed by collapsing on the bed!

Just like the lobby, our room was cool, clean and simply but adequately appointed. We would rest well that night and be refreshed and ready to take on the second leg of our journey to Fort Sill.

The next morning, after a hot meal, we were again on the road. We arrived at the Officer's Guest House at 11:30 p.m., Tuesday, July 28. We were greeted by a sleepy sergeant who confirmed our reservation, checked the location of our car, handed us a "Welcome to Fort Sill" packet, and directed us to our room.

This room was furnished in what could be described as "old military." There were two mahogany twin beds, a mahogany dresser and chest, two overstuffed chairs with a mahogany lamp table in between. Two mahogany night stands flanked the beds. Two large Indian-lore prints adorned the walls. Extra olive-drab blankets were stacked on top of the unenclosed closet. The entire scene was one of no frills—but a lot of substance. The hardwood appointments of the room gave us a sense of permanence the moment we arrived. We learned to be comfortable with the military charter of frugality.

Back in April at West Point, the selection process for first assignments had been held and I had chosen Field Artillery. I had become fascinated with Artillery beginning with my cannoneer training at West Point's Camp Buckner training site. My interest had been reinforced during a second-year summer visit to the Army's Field Artillery Center and School located near Lawton, Oklahoma. I had been impressed by the variety of challenges offered by Artillery. There were opportunities to pursue the more pedestrian orientation of an infantry "grunt"—as well as the mobility epitomized by Armor. Artillery ranged from the small-caliber horse-drawn howitzers that relied heavily on manual deployment to highly-mobile lightly armored self-propelled guns. I was also intrigued by the technical fire direction procedures necessary to launch a projectile to a variety of unseen targets located many miles from the firing position. Target acquisition using distance measuring, optical, and directional equipment was another aspect of Artillery that fascinated me.

I had been assigned to the 4th Field Artillery Battalion (Pack)—the Army's last horse-drawn artillery unit—located at Camp Carson, Colorado. However, before I could start that assignment, all cadets who selected Field Artillery had to attend a 15-week Basic Officer Course designed to provide hands-on Field Artillery training in particular as well as development of fundamental skills needed by junior officers of the Army in general.

The next day after arriving at Fort Sill, Lillian and I began looking for an apartment in the nearby town of Lawton, Oklahoma. Post quarters were not provided for students of the Basic Officer Course.

As we began our search, we were shocked. We were well aware of Jim Crow patterns nationwide. But, so far, we had managed to navigate the country without serious incident. Now, Lillian and I were discovering that despite Truman's order outlawing racial discrimination in the armed forces—old habits die hard.

For the most part, my classmates at Fort Sill carefully avoided any discussion of their living arrangements or the virtues of one area of Lawton versus another. All of the "colored" elite lived on one block within the "Negro" area of Lawton. They were fiercely proud of the special status they enjoyed and were not inclined to expand their circle to fellow travelers who showed up in the area for short stays. To me, their snobbery was sadly comedic and just as offensive as the mindless bigotry of avowed racists. After two days of apartment shopping and finding nothing reasonably habitable available for blacks, I had decided to go to the appropriate authorities and appeal for a special dispensation to allow us to live on Post.

But Lillian was always an optimist. She advised me against asking for any dispensation. "Something will turn up," she told me.

Just before throwing caution to the wind and marching into an office to state our case, I learned of a new colored apartment complex being constructed on the edge of the city. Better yet, these Council Heights Apartments were just as they were described to us, with one notable exception! They were comfortable and affordable—by far the best accommodations available to us. That is, except for our neighbor: a meat-packing plant. A foul odor permeated the entire neighborhood but, by this time, Lillian and I felt we needed to settle somewhere. "We'll get used to the smell," she reassured me.

I nodded. What else could I do? We had no other viable option. "At least the price is right for this place," I told her.

The apartment we rented at 635 B Street was new and furnished with cheap modern furniture. We had a corner apartment, which we liked. Nearly all of our neighbors were either students at Fort Sill or part of the Post Cadre. We quickly made friends with most of our neighbors and settled in for the duration of my schooling.

The Basic Officer Course was designed to teach each new second lieutenant the basic skills of firing battery duties, staff functions, fire direction, target acquisition, communications and equipment maintenance. The course consisted of a minimal amount of formal podium instruction with heavy focus on classroom drills, followed by commensurate practical application in the field. While not officially acknowledged as such, the Gunnery Department was the first among equals within the Field Artillery School. All Field Artillery disciplines converged on the primary mission of providing accurate and timely fire support to the ground gaining arms—hence the primacy of the Gunnery Department.

The class was divided into groups of 20. Each group was under the supervision of an Army or Marine Corps gunnery officer, usually a captain or first lieutenant who was an expert at field artillery—along with good communications skills. A Marine Corps first lieutenant was my gunnery instructor. The lieutenant exuded confidence and made no secret of his desire to prove that he was equal to the best the Army had to offer. He had determined that his would be the best class of all. We felt the pressure and it motivated all of us. Delivery of on-time, accurate and effective fire depended upon the integration of communications, weapons, target acquisition and surveillance. On a given day, my group might be assigned to the firing batteries. Our next assignment could be the development of firing data in the Fire Direction Center. Or, we might be assigned to observation posts in order to locate targets and make necessary firing volley adjustments leading to what was called "firing for effect." On still other occasions, our primary purpose would be to maneuver and maintain the myriad of equipment integral to Field Artillery. Each of these disciplines was a subset of what ultimately was called a directed multi-faceted indirect fire system, the effectiveness of which would be measured by live firing on typical artillery targets.

The course culminated in a massive firepower demonstration that began by parading all of our Field Artillery equipment past a viewing stand for our colleagues, families, local dignitaries as well as the commanding general, his staff and the faculty of the school. Then, all of our equipment was deployed under simulated battlefield conditions. The Armor and Infantry companies assigned to Fort Sill for school support kicked off the demonstration with a fire-and-maneuver exercise featuring all of their small arms, tanks and mortars. Air support was provided by a fighter squadron from nearby Tinker Air Force Base. Immediately following, firing batteries equipped with 75 mm howitzers, the smallest-caliber cannon, were demonstrated. Then came 105 mm howitzer batteries in a sequence that progressed all the way up to 8-inch howitzers. The staggered thunder-like reports of the distant pieces reached the viewing stands with a frequency determined by the gun locations, causing ominous "whooshes" of projectiles as they passed overhead en route to the target area.

The whole demonstration was dramatically narrated for the crowd, culminating in a simultaneous hammering of the battlefield using all available artillery and air support. The narrator declared triumphantly: "Nothing could survive such a blanket of steel!"

My classmates and I chuckled knowingly. In the nearby woods, two deer pranced through the dust and debris, completely unhurt.

Life on the base was going well and so was life on the home front. Lillian had adapted well to her role as an Army wife. She did not question the demands on my time. When I was at home, it was quality time made sweeter by her commitment to this new life we were forging together. Our limited opportunities for social interaction made our apartment the focal point of our lives. Lillian was an immaculate housekeeper with a

God-given sense of taste. At least, that was our impression of our home-life because of an uncanny melding of both likes and dislikes. Whether shopping for gifts, clothes, furniture or whatever, we seemed to converge on the same items. I always looked forward to coming home. Lillian made it so.

Lillian also got her first taste of Army protocol. She easily accepted the mandatory requirement for attendance at certain social events we all referred to as "command performances." The usually muted atmosphere of these occasions suited both of us. Except for wine sometimes served at these affairs, we did not drink. We made no apologies for our straitlaced behavior. We were happy with ourselves and felt privileged just to be a part of such company. We may have been considered dull by some, but I also had the sense that we were respected for our confidence and reserve in such social settings.

I graduated in the top third of my class. All members of BOC 53-1 except a few who failed to meet academic requirements were now branch-qualified and ready to make their first Permanent Change of Station (PCS). For the West Point and ROTC contingents, this would effectively mark the beginning of our military careers.

Fort Sill had been a confidence builder for Lillian and me. I was now ready to tackle whatever challenges I would face as a member of the 4th Field Artillery (Pack). The 4th was one of the oldest outfits in the Army, steeped in long tradition. They had tenaciously resisted many changes in the modern Army, resulting in a unique Table of Organization and Equipment (TOE). That's the formal name of the chart that specifies organization, staffing, and equipment of Army units. In the 4th, horses and mules were still a part of the TOE as the burden bearers and prime movers of their 75 mm howitzers and supporting equipment. During World War II, the battalion had fought in the Italian Alps and openly boasted that there was no place that they could not go. They considered themselves to be a breed apart rather than accept the widely held view that they were a dying breed. They were to the Field Artillery what the Horse Cavalry had been to Armor—a fiercely proud remnant hanging on more as a monument to the past than a serious contributor in any future conflict.

Lillian and I departed Fort Sill early on Monday November 11, 1953, bound for Camp Carson. We were thinking of the excitement of this next chapter in our lives. We weren't too concerned that our itinerary took us westward to Amarillo, Texas, north and west through New Mexico, and ultimately to Colorado Springs, Colorado. We knew where we were headed this time. There was no family housing available at Camp Carson, but we already had planned for temporary lodging in a private home in Colorado Springs. Our host had agreed that we could arrive at any hour, so we decided to drive straight through to our destination. That was the most sensible way for a black couple to travel in those days through regions where we had no family or friends.

The first several hundred miles were somewhat tedious, but not unpleasant. We had lots to talk about from our time at Fort Sill—as well as our hopes for this new posting. Eventually, we reached a little sleepy town called Clayton, New Mexico. It was just before evening fell, and we stopped for fuel at a local gas station and asked about a place to eat. The young attendant recommended a nearby restaurant.

I thought it was obvious that we were looking for a place that allowed colored patronage, so I was unprepared for the reception. Pulling into the parking lot, I began to suspect this was not an establishment that welcomed patrons like me. Today, minority households make up a quarter of Clayton's population—but this was more than half a century ago.

I took a deep breath and turned off the engine. We were hungry. It was getting late.

Then, I warned Lillian to stay in the car while I went inside. "Let me make a test run," I told her. This time, she nodded and sat silently as I walked toward the front door.

Even before I reached the door, I could hear the sounds of boisterous storytelling and knee-slapping humor. I looked back at Lillian, then squared my shoulders and pulled open the door.

That cheery wave of voices crashed into an ominous silence. All eyes, including those of the colored bus boy, were fixed on me. Suddenly, everyone—including me—understood that this was a remarkable event. My first instinct was to whirl on my heel and leave.

But, I was committed. I had cautiously left Lillian in the relative safety of the car, so I decided to step confidently up to the counter. Several steps later, I was not so sure this was a smart course of action.

Every soul in the place waited for what would happen next. On cue, as if playing what she must have assumed was her role in this drama, a waitress poured all the disgust she could muster into a question: "What do you want? *Boy*."

The room erupted in a chorus of ominous murmuring.

I considered blurting out: Nothing! But, as I say, I was committed. I told that waitress: "Three hamburgers and two large Cokes to go."

She was outraged by my apparent confidence and turned up the contempt with a loudly slurred, "*Nigras* is served at the back *doh*. You have to go 'round to the back *doh*!"

Before I could react, the owner suddenly appeared and told the waitress, "Just give him what he wants." By no means was he friendly toward me. Clearly, he simply wanted to contain an explosive situation before someone ignited the fuel.

The waitress made a grand show of incredulity at this instruction, followed by a flurry of activity that made it obvious to every patron that this was the most distasteful task that she had ever been forced to execute.

Now, the room began to stir. Two men stood and without any audible exchange moved menacingly toward the door.

Another voice resounded from the back of the room with a snarling, "Well, somebody opened the *doh*—didn't *dey*!?!" Others began to chime in with colloquialisms aimed at intimidating me and arousing the crowd.

The waitress threw the food toward me. As I was paying the bill, I could hear the scrubbing of chair legs on the floor as every man in the place pushed away from his table. They rose in unison.

Looking neither to the left nor to the right, I tried to appear unruffled. I felt the strange sensation of the floor seemingly moving beneath my feet, drawing me back into the restaurant even as I tried to leave that place. As I passed through the front door, I noticed a pickup truck approaching slowly. Nearing our car, I could see Lillian looking anxiously in my direction. As I silently slid in behind the wheel, an overwhelming stream of emotions consumed me.

Anger! Fear! And finally, I was consumed by rage, absolute fury that we were being subjected to … to what exactly? This incident was not over. I wasn't the only one leaving the place. Patrons were getting into their cars. I could hear engine after engine roaring to life. Suddenly, helplessness trumped all other concerns. I had no way to call for police protection. Clearly, I could not count on anyone coming to our rescue. Given the prevailing system of justice, the local sheriff might well have been in the first vehicle lining up behind us.

Lillian said nothing, as if breaking the silence would unleash whatever sinister forces her intuition told her were rising all around us.

Now, the entire parking lot and a surrounding field were illuminated by headlights as the patrons revved their engines. Then, they blinked those lights. On. Off. On.

I started our car and eased onto the highway. Looking through the rearview mirror, I saw their convoy right behind us. As I rounded a curve in the road, I could see the long line of trailing headlights. I was now convinced that our pursuers were on the verge of forcing us off the road.

But, I was committed. There was nothing I could do but grip the wheel and drive.

Finally, after a couple of miles, I could look back and see headlights turning left and right behind me. I drove on.

I can't recall how far I was from the restaurant when the last headlights turned away. One thing we certainly understood without another word passing between us: We would not stop again until we reached Colorado Springs. Lillian and I knew that, as we crisscrossed the country I had pledged to serve, not every community was as welcoming as the little havens we had enjoyed at West Point or in Detroit or even on Martha's Vineyard.

Jim Crow was alive and well in America.

6

Could I Shoot?

*My country wants to be constructive, not destructive. It wants agreements,
not wars, among nations. It wants to live in freedom and in the
confidence that the people of every other nation enjoy equally the right
of choosing their own way of life. So, my country's purpose is to help us
move out of this dark chamber of horrors into the light, to find a way by
which the minds of men, the hopes of men, the souls of men everywhere,
can move forward toward peace and happiness and well-being.*

**From President Dwight D. Eisenhower's "Atoms for Peace"
address at the United Nations, December 8, 1953**

When we rolled into Colorado Springs, its population was just one-tenth
of today's half a million. But, that little town high in the Rockies already
had deep international roots. The Colorado Gold Rush of 1858 drew
hopeful miners from around the world, shouting the slogan: "Pikes Peak
or Bust!" By the 1970s, the U.S. Olympic Committee chose the town for
its new national headquarters.

As we finally parked our car well after midnight, Lillian and I were still
shaken by our escape from the restaurant. So, we were thrilled that the
owners of our temporary lodgings warmly greeted us. They didn't mind
the late arrival. They seemed delighted to have young tenants. The last of
their own children had left the nest a year earlier.

The next day, we were determined to explore the town. Near dinnertime,
we dared to ask the manager of a local drugstore to recommend a place
to eat. Without hesitation, he directed us to a restaurant in downtown
Colorado Springs. As we pulled into that parking area, I felt a surge of
anxiety, but managed to disguise my uneasiness from Lillian. As it turned
out, we had found yet another hospitable haven in America's complex
landscape of diversity and exclusivity. A smiling hostess quickly dispelled
my apprehensions and welcomed us as valued customers. The food was

superb. The ambiance was comfortable. The staff seemed to function as a supportive community. In fact, the owner's wife ranged between inquisitive and nosey as she peppered us with questions. As soon as she learned about my assignment to Camp Carson, which was just 8 miles to the south, she wanted to know about where we planned to stay. Before dinner was over, she had called a friend to ask about a rental vacancy. Her friend was aware of the recent refurbishment of an old mansion for the purpose of converting it into apartments. The trauma of the previous day's experience was now beginning to wane. In the afterglow of a good meal and promising prospects for housing, we recounted our experiences in St. Louis and Clayton and concluded that nothing is as bad as it seems and everything that happens must be kept in perspective. We were definitely upbeat as we left the restaurant. Come what may, we would be equal to it!

The next day we made an appointment to visit the place recommended by the proprietor of the restaurant. We arrived at 615 North Corona promptly at 10 a.m. The massive old frame house was located in an attractive Colorado Springs neighborhood and covered most of a triangular shaped island. We were immediately impressed by its stately Victorian appearance. It had been freshly painted white with green trim. We were not sure which of four access doors to enter to meet the owner. Much to our surprise, the proprietor was a black woman who welcomed us in a manner that was all business. Lillian was thrilled with the quality and tastefulness of the furniture. The second-floor apartment she showed us extended over the rear of the building with only a single wall contiguous with another apartment, so we would have a sense of privacy. The price was right. The location was ideal for easy access to downtown Colorado Springs and Camp Carson. Our apartment would be available in three days, which would give us ample time to settle in before I had to report for duty. When left alone to further explore the nooks and crannies of her new home, Lillian hugged me and again did her joyous pirouette. The trauma of Clayton, New Mexico, was fading fast.

When I arrived at Camp Carson, I found the commanding officer to be an intimidating presence behind a large mahogany desk flanked on each side by the U.S. and 4th Field Artillery Battalion (Pack) flags.

I crisply saluted as I announced: "Lt. Worthy reporting for duty, sir!"

The battalion commander returned the salute and quickly surveyed me from head to toe.

"Sit down, lieutenant," he said with an aura of authority that signaled this would be a no-nonsense encounter.

The 4th field commander had come up through the ranks to lead one of the Army's elite units. Along the way he had built a stable group of influential military and civilian contacts and was highly regarded as a soldier but was not considered to be in the mainstream of modern Army thinking. He was a proud man but entertained no illusions about stars in his future.

He dispensed with the usual preliminary small talk and got right to the point, asking me, "Why do you want to sign up with the 4th Field?"

I had anticipated his question but did not immediately appreciate the subtlety of its wording, which did not acknowledge the fact that I had already been assigned to the 4th. I responded: "Field Artillery has always been my first choice and when I learned about the 4th and its unique operations and history, I liked the challenge and wanted to be a part of it."

"Do you have any experience with animals?"

"No sir," and I had planned to add that I was eager to learn—but the colonel abruptly cut me off.

"I hate to disappoint you, lieutenant, but it wouldn't be in your best interest to assign you to my outfit for several reasons. One, you probably won't learn anything except how to take care of mules. Two, the future of the 4th is doubtful. Technology is passing us by. We're on the backside of the power curve." Then, he paused as if nothing else needed to be said, but he wasn't sure that I comprehended the full import of his message.

I clearly understood, and my first reaction was the trivial reflection that his promised "several reasons" had dwindled to two. The colonel uncharacteristically rambled on about the lack of mission definition, outmoded equipment, and other ancillary arguments supporting the probability of the demise of Pack Artillery. Then, he told me, "Your orders have been changed to assign you to the 547th Armored Field Artillery Battalion here at Camp Carson."

I maintained my composure, but was puzzled and disappointed at this turn of events. Because of the unique capabilities of the Army's only Pack Artillery unit, I had suspected that as a black officer, I would be breaking new ground. I also knew that one of my classmates had also selected the 4th, and wondered if he too had been redirected to another unit. Yet I also reasoned that the colonel's assessment of my future with the 4th, if sincere, made sense. I diplomatically expressed my disappointment but indicated that I understood the long-term implications and looked forward to my new assignment. The colonel wished me good luck and turned me over to his adjutant for direction to the Armored Guardian—the 547th Armored Field Artillery Battalion.

I never saw a mule.

Lillian was preparing her first full meal at our new apartment when I returned from my encounter with the 4th field commander. My ambivalence towards the outcome of my session with the colonel had not touched off any discernable mood swing. I simply was surprised and puzzled and wondering what lay ahead with this sudden change. Lillian was so eager to share this first meal that she did not directly inquire about my new assignment. I was focused on the culinary delights, too, so it actually took a while before I finally blurted out: "My orders assigning me to the 4th Field have been revoked."

"What happened?"

"I've been reassigned to an armored artillery outfit called the 547th AFA."

"Why?"

"The colonel said, in effect, that the 4th was a relic of the past and I wouldn't learn anything except how to handle mules."

Lillian's response was tempered by her personal philosophy that advocated disengagement from those events over which one had no control. "The colonel was right," she said. "You don't want to start your career with a loser."

I needed that. That immediate reassurance from Lillian removed any lingering concern that I might have been shortchanged on what I had been promised.

Once again, my life had changed in 24 hours. I soon learned that I was the first black officer assigned to the 547th Armored Field Artillery. The 547th consisted of Headquarters Battery, Service Battery, and three Firing Batteries called A, B and C. Headquarters Battery furnished administrative support for the battalion staff. Service Battery provided the additional maintenance and logistics support required by the three identical firing batteries. I had been posted to A Battery as an assistant executive officer. My battery commander was Capt. William Boiler, West Point class of 1945.

I was joining A Battery in the middle of preparations for their Annual Training Test. This test was taken by each of the firing batteries to measure proficiency in performing the unit's basic mission of providing direct fire support to ground forces. I assumed the additional duty of forward observer for the battery test. This was a daunting challenge, because Boiler was easily the most competent of all the battery commanders. His battery executive officers were responsible for the reconnaissance, selection and occupation of firing positions. A heavily weighted portion of the test measured my ability to tactically occupy an observation post overlooking the target area, locate designated targets, communicate that location to the fire direction center, and make the necessary volley adjustments to bring effective live fire on to simulated enemy personnel and installations. Using appropriate instrumentation, I had to orient six self-propelled howitzers in the firing battery to insure parallel and predictable delivery of 105 mm projectiles to the desired area.

Capt. Boiler accompanied me to observe my first practice selection and wasted no time putting me to the acid test. He wanted to know: could I shoot?

After establishing communications with the fire direction center, Boiler directed me to locate my position on the map and send the coordinates to the fire direction officer (FDO). Boiler then swept the impact area with his battery commander (BC) scope to search for a permanent terrain feature or pre-positioned material suitable to test my ability to adjust fire onto a designated target. Finding a pile of junk in a nondescript area that made distance estimation difficult, even for an experienced observer, Boiler defined the junk as an enemy bunker and ordered me to destroy it.

I fixed the position of the "bunker" using polar coordinates and radioed the fire direction center: "Redeye 3, this is Redeye 5, fire mission, over."

FDO: "Redeye 5, this is Redeye 3, send your mission, over."

I responded: "Azimuth 1750, distance 3000, over,"

FDO: "Azimuth 1750, distance 3000, over."

"Enemy bunker, will adjust, over."

FDO: "Enemy bunker, will adjust, wait."

Knowing my position, the FDO converted the target data into weapons data. The data was then communicated to the firing battery executive officer's post, where it was further refined to allow for weapons peculiarities, distribution, fuse settings, and impact area safety considerations.

I radioed to the FDO: "Battery adjust Shell HE Fuse Quick Center 1 round Deflection 1640 Elevation 340."

Under the supervision of the chief of firing battery, the two center-position howitzers quickly applied the data to their onboard sighting instruments using the pre-oriented aiming stakes for deflection reference and a quadrant for the tube elevation setting.

Upon confirmation of the center platoon's readiness to fire, the battery executive officer commanded: "Fire!", followed by, "On the way," to the FDO.

FDO: "On the way, over."

I responded: "On the way, wait."

I now trained my binoculars onto the anticipated impact point while simultaneously surveying the area surrounding the target in order to assure detection of the adjusting rounds. I saw the impact of the two rounds beyond the bunker and requested: "Drop 200, over."

FDO: "Drop 200, wait."

Boiler also observed the adjusting rounds through his BC scope, which was equipped with optics that provided greater definition of the impact area. He applauded my time-saving and bold adjustment, which deviated from the artillery school recommendation of a more conservative "drop 400" adjustment with its greater assurance of bracketing the target.

FDO: "On the way, over."

I responded: "On the way, wait."

After assuring myself that the next two rounds were short of the target, I requested with some degree of relief: "Add 100, over."

FDO: "Add 100, wait."

FDO: "On the way, over."

I responded: "On the way, wait."

These rounds landed slightly beyond the target, confirming the establishment of a bracket. I called out: "Drop 50, fuse delay, fire for effect, over."

My final adjustment informed the FDO that impact was now within 50 meters of the target, which, by procedure, released the four flanking howitzers to join the center platoon in attacking the target. The change in fuse from one that set off the high explosive on impact to one with a delay feature allowed projectile penetration before explosion. This afforded a greater potential for destroying a reinforced installation like a bunker. The ultimate effect might not have been total destruction, but I had used all the tools at my disposal to accomplish my mission.

Capt. Boiler expressed his approval of my performance with a caustic: "Well done, lieutenant."

Unspoken was his obvious astonishment at my self-assurance and command of established artillery procedures. I could tell that Boiler had not expected much from me. Not only was I a greenhorn lieutenant, but I was also a novelty as the first black officer. After that smashing battery test, Boiler began to realize that he had unjustly stereotyped me. Now, Boiler was jubilant. We got a 97.4 rating out of a possible 100, virtually assuring A Battery's designation as the top firing battery in the 547th. It was also a personal triumph for me. I had played a pivotal role in one of the most critical segments of the test—the ability to place accurate, effective, and timely fire on a target.

This had been my baptism of fire as the only new officer in the battalion. A celebration was in order. Capt. Boiler decided to have a battery party. I wasn't prepared for what followed. Unlike the parties I had been accustomed to, this one was instant fun and frivolity. There was no warm-up period in which revelers gradually got to know one another with the corresponding phase out of inhibitions as the beer took its toll. At this party, there was a steady chorus: "Hiya, lieutenant! Wanna drink?" No hard liquor was served, but there would have been no discernible difference if it had been available. As the evening wore on, there was the constant threat of physical conflict involving various factions of battery enlisted personnel. It seemed as if the party had primed pent-up frustrations of long standing, to the point that there was little or no check on self-control. The first sergeant and the company clerk disappeared for a few minutes, only to return with scratches and bruises from a "fall" that they had jointly experienced. There was an abundance of agitators but no peacemakers. This was a dangerous situation—and I longed for that evening to come to an end. I grew more anxious when Boiler left early. The other officers seemed oblivious to the potential for disaster.

Much to my relief, Lt. Col. Tacklind, the battalion commander, dropped by as a matter of protocol to congratulate the officers and men of A Battery. His appearance restored a modicum of discipline. He huddled with the officers and noncommissioned officers who were still sober enough to pay their respects. An old warrior, but not a strict disciplinarian, Tacklind mingled easily with the troops and was unperturbed by the near chaos that surrounded him. I later reasoned that he had been immunized by the fact that he had nine children of his own. I survived that night without any physical or professional bruises and considered that a success.

Battalion tests followed battery tests. The objectives were essentially the same, except for the escalation of the level of effort and the requirement to integrate fire and movement of the entire battalion. The focus was on the functioning of the battalion staff. Capt. Boiler was relieved of his command and pulled up to become the battalion training and plans officer. He now became the principal advisor to Tacklind on all technical and tactical matters, which were the most heavily weighted areas of the test.

In preparation for the battalion test, Tacklind moved the entire battalion to the field. This was my first participation in battalion operations. Manning a battalion observation post gave me instant exposure and concert with all elements of the staff. Similar recognition would have taken weeks, if not months, under garrison conditions.

I quickly learned battalion strengths and weaknesses, as well as the human factors of this microcosm of the U.S. Army. Maj. Harry Jefferson, battalion executive officer, was a case in point. Ammunition resupply procedures were to be evaluated during the test. Certain forms and tables used to monitor available supply rates had been inadvertently left in Jefferson's field office, which also served as his living quarters while on bivouac. I was dispatched from the field command post to pick up the forms along with other items required by Capt. Boiler. The forms were not in the top drawer of Jefferson's field desk as I had been instructed. Returning without them was unthinkable. I began to search in the logical places, beginning with the other drawers in the desk. In the bottom drawer, wrapped in brown paper, was a fifth of bourbon. I moved from the desk to the file cabinets. Fifths of bourbon were also found in the back of the top drawer of one of the cabinets and in the back of the bottom drawer in the second cabinet. The rear of the top shelf of a bookcase containing field manuals, other documents—and yet another fifth. Finally, I found the ammunition forms! Along the way, I had a good glimpse at a functioning alcoholic's convenient stash of booze. I marveled at Jefferson's ability to function while in his cups.

Harry Jefferson had come up through the ranks based upon his shrewdness and a guileless demeanor. For a while he had kept pace with his contemporaries intellectually but without concern for image or the physical trappings which, though superficial, count so much in the process of recognition and rewards. He knew that he would rise no further and began to internalize a resentment that others with a lesser command of the fundamentals had passed him by. I reasoned that he had taken to the bottle in part to stem a silent rage against a system in which such a premium was placed on dash and dazzle in the Army's portfolio for success.

Jefferson inconspicuously became my mentor. He avoided preferential treatment, but craftily prevented me from being shunted outside the mainstream of the battalion. For my part, I did nothing exceptional to earn Jefferson's allegiance, save treat him with the respect that was his due. Jefferson was determined that he would minimize the impact of color on my career as long as he was a member of the 547th. He took on this challenge partly in retaliation against those who had placed a cap on his own career because he either could not or would not follow the prescription that led to the stars.

His wife was unconventional in her own right. We thought of her affectionately as "the old broad," because she seemed to have stepped out of Hollywood casting for that role. She always wore heavy makeup, had frizzy hair and spoke in a deep, raspy voice. Lillian and I agreed that everything about her exterior seemed to belie her inner beauty. Lillian first met Mrs. Jefferson at a gathering for the battalion officers' wives, hosted by Mrs. Tacklind. These "coffees" were the favored protocol for wives to socialize in a separate but parallel process to the way their husbands were forming bonds in daily service. Usually, a coffee was a dress-up affair, where finger food was served with an accompanying activity such as a fashion show, guest speaker or a presentation designed to acquaint wives with some aspect of the battalion's mission. In contrast to Mrs. Tacklind's genteel elegance, Mrs. Jefferson talked too much, too loudly—and always showed up in clothing that seemed to harken from some earlier era.

It was no accident that Lillian shared a table with Mrs. Jefferson at their first coffee together. Harry Jefferson's interest in me had prompted his wife to reach out to Lillian. Mrs. Jefferson clearly was no respecter of persons. She treated everyone the same—never a hidden agenda. Exalting rank or social standing was contemptible to her. Lillian appreciated her candor and enjoyed her absolute authenticity. They quickly became friends even as Lillian was receiving her introduction to Mrs. Jefferson's alcohol dependency, which nearly equaled that of her husband's.

Mrs. Jefferson was generous to a fault. Her salty exterior concealed an innate softness and sensitivity toward welcoming others. She loved to lounge about in satin and lace and show off her collection of figurines. She made it clear that her "Jeff" enjoyed first place in her life, with her miniature poodle a close second. Lillian quickly came to love this older woman's warm friendship, even though the Jefferson household was always in a state of laughable disarray. This warm friendship allowed Lillian to enjoy the best of two worlds. She now had a surrogate mother who provided fire-tested maternal support while allowing Lillian to sort out and reject the untidy aspects of her friend's value system. Lillian longed to appropriate Mrs. Jefferson's ability to project such welcoming warmth. From Mrs. Jefferson, she learned that real freedom that comes from being true to oneself. But there was a downside to their relationship that would plague Lillian the rest of her life. Mrs. Jefferson's loosely wrapped approach to life, often leaving messes in her wake, catalyzed Lillian's insatiable, impossible quest for perfection in her own life.

We loved our life at Camp Carson, so there was quite a shock when Lillian and I each discovered fateful news on the same day. I had discovered that—as part of an Army-wide austerity and realignment program—the 547th was ordered to relocate from Camp Carson to Fort Knox, Kentucky. When I learned of the pending move, I telephoned Lillian to tell her that I had some news that I would share with her later that evening. Lillian seemed almost oblivious to my promised revelation as she announced that she too would have news for me.

As soon as I entered the parlor of our apartment that evening, I dramatically led Lillian to the sofa. "Guess what?" I began. "The whole battalion is moving to Fort Knox. The word came down today. We will be part of an armor group."

Lillian asked, "When do we leave?"

I replied, "In mid-July—about six weeks from now."

Lillian murmured wistfully, "I guess the baby will be born in Kentucky."

I bolted up, gazed expectantly into Lillian's eyes and waited for her to explain. When she smiled but said nothing, I was sure of what she meant, but my eyes begged for those specific words of affirmation.

Finally, she said, "I'm pregnant."

Suddenly, I realized there was only one item of news that day. "How—" I began, then could not manage to speak for a moment. I began again, "When?" And, before Lillian could answer that question, I stammered, "Are—are you sure?"

"Yes."

We had planned to delay beginning a family until a year after we were married. It had been almost a year to the day, but I had given no further thought to having children before that moment. I grinned and lifted Lillian off the sofa, whirled her around, stopped, and in a voice about two octaves higher than normal, asked, "Why didn't you tell me?"

"I did as soon as I knew for sure."

The rest of the evening was spent revisiting and reaffirming our commitment to each other and recasting our future. We became immersed in a world of our own creation—a world in which positives always overcame negatives and greatness was predestined for those who refused to accept anything less. We reasoned that if we created him (we had decided that the firstborn should be a boy), our nurturing rights provided an insuperable advantage over any external forces in shaping the course of his future. Our child would not be caged by the constraints of the world. His character and values would neutralize the barriers of race, class and culture. It was inconceivable to us that God might contravene a plan so consistent with what He intended for everyone.

I soon learned that I was selected for the advance party preceding the move of the main body of the 547th to Fort Knox. Prior to our departure to Kentucky, I had to supervise the loading of the tracked vehicles onto flatcars for rail shipment to Fort Knox. This proved to be a major logistics challenge. Extensive coordination with the servicing rail system involved determination of the number and type of cars needed, spotting of the cars for optimum accessibility, securing tie-down tools and materials—plus a whole host of complex safety requirements. Thanks in large part to the superb leadership of Sgt. 1st Class Richardson, the chief of firing battery, movement of the vehicles to the railyard and subsequent loading went without a hitch.

The success of this assignment was marred by a tragic mishap, which occurred after the vehicles had been secured and consigned to the rail company. One of the cannoneers independently decided to ship some personal items with the rail shipment. Without authorization, he drove to the rail marshalling area, climbed aboard his assigned howitzer and was killed instantly as his body made contact with an overhead power line. This would be the first of several line-of-duty tragedies I would encounter throughout my career.

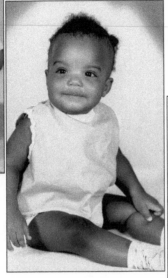
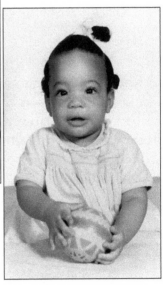

Mark, Kym, Jennifer.

7

Revelations

*For nothing is hidden that will not be disclosed, nor is anything
secret that will not become known and come to light.*

Luke 8:17

You don't choose your family. They are God's gift to you, as you are to them.

Desmond Tutu

A whole host of events unfolded in the 1950s with historic implications we
could not even guess as they occurred. By 1955, when Lillian and I arrived
at Fort Knox, global events were moving at a nuclear pace. In mid-January,
that year, a crowd in Groton, Connecticut celebrated the launch of the
USS Nautilus, our first nuclear-powered submarine. That same week, the
Pentagon announced plans to develop intercontinental ballistic missiles
(ICBMs) armed with nuclear weapons. In 1955, President Eisenhower
sent the first American advisors to South Vietnam; Marian Anderson
became the first African-American singer to perform at the Metropolitan
Opera in New York City; Ray Kroc opened his first McDonald's in Des
Plaines, Illinois; and Walt Disney opened the gates to Disneyland in Ana-
heim, California. Our American landscape was changing dramatically!

On the ground at Fort Knox, I was still mourning the needless loss of
one of our men before we even got on the road. I was also overwhelmed
with preparations for the arrival of the main body of our forces.

Our orders were clear. We had to:

- Establish liaison with the armor group that would be the parent
  organization.

- Accept and assign facilities to all elements of the battalion based
  upon organizational and tactical considerations.

- Inspect and receive equipment needed to house, feed and assure the combat readiness of the officers and men of the 547th.
- Allocate family housing and identify services and facilities dedicated to the well-being of dependents.
- Receive the main body upon their arrival into their designated area at Fort Knox.

Because of my preoccupation with my mission, Lillian took responsibility for reconnoitering the Post on her own. While she had loved our apartment in Colorado Springs, she was thrilled at the prospect of living on Post. She felt that she could now fully embrace her role as an Army wife—what Mrs. Jefferson had often wistfully described as the Army family. The commissary, Post Exchange, hospital and other ancillary facilities of one of the Army's major installations would be at Lillian's immediate disposal. Whatever anxieties she had harbored after I informed her of the move were neutralized as she gazed across the lush landscape of Fort Knox and checked out the Officers Club.

However, permanent quarters were not immediately available. All newly arriving, married lieutenants were temporarily assigned to a high-rise efficiency apartment building called Newgarden Apartments. It was here that we met Ruth and Dave Jones. Hailing from Kirkwood, Missouri, Ruth and Dave were also newlyweds who had recently been assigned to the 547th. Dave was a 1953 ROTC graduate from the University of Missouri. Ruth had been his sweetheart since high school days. They described themselves as growing up WASP with no real contact with "colored people," except for a maid when Dave was a child. Now, thanks to the Army system, we wound up in adjoining apartments.

Dave and Ruth were bright, high-spirited products of families of some means. Both had been nurtured in environments that engendered independence and self-worth. Initially, we thought the Joneses to be aggressive in building the relationship of our foursome, but the cultural reticence on the part of Lillian and me quickly succumbed to the warmth and sincerity of Dave and "Ruthie." We became inseparable. Their friendship transcended all barriers, no matter the origin. It was this encounter that shaped our future outlook toward whites—an attitude that predisposed us toward trust and acceptance.

Dave was awestruck by my West Point experience; I was equally fascinated by Dave's openness and adaptability. Initially, we held back a little of ourselves to cushion the letdown just in case Dave and Ruthie were not for real. We quickly learned that with this couple—what you saw was what you got.

Dave and I were assigned to separate firing batteries, which led to a friendly rivalry, as well as an opportunity to realize the synergism that came from sharing techniques unique to the personalities of our respective outfits. There was never an end to the dialogue between us about our professional challenges—and, of course, our shared fanatic interest in sports. Our friendship remained strong even after we were assigned to permanent quarters. The Jones' Nash Rambler was parked in front of our home at 161 H Pritchard Place as often as it was parked at their own home on Patton Drive. Lillian and Ruthie bonded as well, especially around Lillian's pregnancy. Lillian and Ruthie complemented each other. Lillian was the organizer who liked to stick to a plan; Ruthie preferred to do things simply because they were fun. Ruthie was full of fresh ideas—some of which conflicted with others. As they shared the planning for our new baby, Lillian visualized the baby's needs in every detail and agonized over the possibility that all arrangements might not be perfect. To Ruthie, the preliminaries should be enjoyed as much as the main event.

On the day Lillian's labor pains began, I was on a field training exercise. Ruthie drove her to Reynolds Army Hospital. At precisely 10:30 a.m., March 14, 1955, Mark Eric Worthy presented himself. I managed to arrive at the hospital at the moment of birth.

Obviously exhausted, Lillian's only words were: "Do you like him?"

"You made him," I said. "How could I not like him?"

Lillian immediately drifted off to sleep. Her uncustomary listlessness caused me to wonder about the difficulty of delivery, so I sought out the attending physician with my questions. He told me that Mark would remain in an incubator as a precaution for a few days, but that we should not expect any lasting complications. I was puzzled at first. I had not even noticed that Mark was born with an extra digit on each of his hands.

Five days later, Lillian was released from the hospital. Mark's sixth fingers had been removed with only slight scars remaining that in time would completely disappear. Otherwise, he was a beautiful, well-formed baby who appeared to be much older than he was. Hardly noticeable was the breadth of the bridge of his nose and the prominence of the upper portion of his head. His early days were uneventful. We were delighted. He was growing strikingly more handsome each day and Lillian never looked or felt better. Dave and Ruthie adored Mark and enthusiastically filled the role of extended family. They later confessed that they had intensified their own efforts to start a family as a result of their experience with Mark.

We had no anxieties other than the daily challenges faced by all new parents. My work became more challenging as I was appointed executive officer of A Battery of the 547th. That's how I met a new battery commander, who I will simply call Harry. He had only recently been cleared for command after having spent two years as a POW in the Korean conflict. Harry was one of a number of officers recently repatriated. All had to go through courts martial proceedings in order to be formally cleared of any complicity with their captors. That kind of formal judicial vindication was seen as an effective way to let these men restart their military careers with a clean slate. All of them had spent a considerable amount of time traveling from trial to trial testifying on behalf of each other.

However, it quickly became obvious to me that Harry's ordeal had taken its toll. He readily, almost eagerly, talked about the terrors of his captivity, displaying a peculiar kind of bravado that wallowed in all the grisly details. Despite his claims to the contrary, I could see that his trials and tribulations had totally stripped him of self-confidence. His self-esteem had been sustained only by his link to the POW fraternity reinforced by months of restoration and rehabilitation once he returned to the states.

He was battery commander in name only. At Harry's behest, I was constantly at his side, even to the extent of riding in his jeep. Every operational decision, no matter how trivial, had to receive my concurrence. My direct and extensive participation in staff meetings was in stark contrast to my counterparts from other batteries, who generally sat passively along the wall for backup purposes only—if indeed they were present at all. Despite my best efforts to keep from upstaging Harry, my attempts to remain in a secondary role in the conduct of A Battery soon became transparent to battalion leadership and rank and file alike.

During the entire time of my association with Harry, there was only one occasion in which he seemed to step up to his responsibility as a commander. That involved the unexpected death of a platoon sergeant after a short illness. Harry took the unprecedented step of transporting the entire battery to the sergeant's homesite and personally supervised an elaborate graveside ceremony. Suddenly and curiously, Harry had become the consummate leader. He took charge of every detail. I reasoned that his POW experience had somehow uniquely equipped him to step up in moments of tragedy. For him, death had become a familiar and strangely comfortable circumstance.

Harry perplexed me in many other ways. He consistently avoided contact with any of the other officers in the battalion. When he learned of my interest in jazz, there was an abrupt change in our relationship—at least from his end. Harry eagerly invited me to his apartment to check out his record collection. I respectfully declined. I had no desire to extend our relationship beyond official obligations.

One Friday morning, Harry called in to report that he was ill and requested me to bring the Morning Report—the daily record of events and unit status—to his apartment for his signature. When I arrived, I realized that his real agenda had little to do with battery business. After futilely pleading with me to have a drink, he launched into an almost frenzied monologue on the virtues of jazz's most distinguished virtuosos. I was amazed at the ease with which he talked about jazz. The Jekyll of the indecisive commander had turned into a Hyde of self-confidence. I was dumbfounded by his sudden attempt to break down all barriers of rank or status between us. I also wondered how he would be able to reconcile all of this on Monday, when the realities of our formal duties resumed. I hastily made an excuse and left before things got completely out of hand.

On Monday, Harry did not show up for duty. I assumed that he was still claiming to be ill and so I covered for him, as I had often done in the past. Included with that day's mail was a large brown envelope incorrectly addressed to the commanding officer, Battery A, 547th AFA Battalion. There were no other markings—nothing to indicate that I was not entitled to know its contents. Inside was a report concerning Harry that actually was intended for the battalion commander's eyes only. The cover letter with several supporting attachments was written in summary sheet format—so the bottom-line conclusion was obvious to me even at a glance. Harry was accused of homosexual activity.

I read no further. My first reaction was not so much shock from the discovery as it was dismay over the manner in which it was discovered. I experienced a wide range of reactions, starting with anger over the carelessness of the sender who had mislabeled the envelope, then moving on to embarrassment over the violation of Harry's privacy. Then, I had the daunting challenge of figuring out how to get this envelope into Lt. Col. Tacklind's hands without further compromise.

I immediately called to verify his availability.

When I arrived, he welcomed me. "Come in lieutenant. How are things going?" Then, without waiting for an answer, Tacklind launched into a dissertation on battalion readiness referring frequently to a recent group directive defining minimum standards.

I struggled to maintain my composure as I waited for an opening to drop the bomb.

Finally, I could wait no longer. "Excuse me, sir, I think this was intended for you."

Tacklind immediately sensed the drama in my demeanor. He took the envelope, opened it and began to read. Within moments, he looked up at me as grim-faced as I had ever seen him. He asked, "Anyone else see this?"

"No sir."

"Thank you, lieutenant, I'll take it from here." I never saw Harry again.

That was one kind of revelation that shook my assumptions about military service. I had never encountered such a case before, but the Uniform Code of Military Justice that Harry Truman had signed into law two years after his order integrating the armed forces left no room for anyone credibly charged with homosexuality.

Another revelation came just after Christmas that year and, unlike the misaddressed envelope that held a thunderclap of news, this truth emerged slowly in our home. Lillian and I were proud parents who basked in wonderment over Mark's evolving good looks as he moved through his first year. We were thankful that he was a good baby—almost too good, with docile behavior that we initially thought was a blessing. Then, at Christmas, we fell into the parental folly of turning Santa Claus into a mirror of our own expectations. In our high spirits, we bought too many toys, too expensive, too advanced and did not realize how inappropriate some of these gifts would be for any infant. The handmade caboose we wrapped up for Mark was more a work of art than a plaything to be yanked about on a string and banged around the house. Like so many parents, we wound up chiding ourselves for our overindulgence in Christmas shopping. Mark was more interested in the wrapping paper than in the contents of the gift boxes! His favorite toy turned out to be a stuffed caterpillar from Dave and Ruthie. Any educational toys, especially those intended to develop motor skills, were quickly abandoned. This was the first real evidence we saw of issues that would unfold in Mark's formative years.

The troubling memory of Mark's first Christmas led to our emerging suspicion that all might not be well with Mark. We weren't willing to acknowledge it, but Lillian and I would catch each other pensively staring at Mark. Neither of us said anything. Both of us feared that any attempt to articulate these suspicions would have seemed absurd to the other. But, eventually we had to admit that Mark seemed especially slow in learning to propel himself. When on his stomach, he could barely hold up his head and turned over with great difficulty. No amount of coaxing had any effect.

"He's just waiting," I remember saying. "He'll take off when he's good and ready."

However, by the time Mark reached his first birthday, hope for the predicted spurt in his development was waning fast. He could only scoot along on his stomach. Lillian devoted herself to endless sessions, coaxing Mark to move and celebrating any progress. She often left little time to cook and do the basic chores before I came home. I would take up the torch as soon as I had properly greeted Lillian and conferred with her about the day's progress. I would likely start by putting Mark on the floor and moving away from him while dangling some enticement, usually the stuffed caterpillar we had dubbed Lenny. After weeks of this, we began to admit that nothing was working.

All aversion to seeking professional help vanished when Lillian unexpectedly announced that she was pregnant again. I immediately made an appointment with Mark's doctor, who initiated a series of tests. His initial evaluations were inconclusive, so periodic reviews were scheduled. The process dragged on until an impending relocation prompted us to press the doctor to draw some conclusions. I was being reassigned, yet again, this time to Fort Sill, Oklahoma, with temporary duty en route at Fort Benning, Georgia, for the purpose of attending airborne "jump" school.

Finally, the doctor wrote up a report of his observations as Mark reached 17 months. Mark was physically healthy, for the most part, but had clearly shown "a slow mental development." The lengthy report detailed a wide range of scans and tests, then ended with ominous words for us: "Clinical Impression: Mental Retardation of Unknown Cause."

Recommendation: This patient's father is being transferred to Fort Sill, Oklahoma. It is recommended that he be followed by the pediatric department with examinations and mental testing when age permits."

We were not completely surprised. We had seen our own signs for months. The doctor had been consulting with us all along—but the cold text of that report hit us as devastating confirmation.

We asked the questions all parents ask after such a report: Why Mark? Why us? Then, we resolved to focus on the important question: Where do we go from here?

I was surprised that our mutual reaction was a squaring of our jaws as we each struggled to come to terms with the news. Now, we would have to factor the special "impact on Mark" into every aspect of our lives.

8

Stand in the Door. Jump!

I am an Airborne trooper! I jump by parachute from any plane in flight. I volunteered to do it, knowing full well the hazards of my choice.

The Airborne Creed

Life in the 20th century is like a parachute jump:
You have to get it right the first time.

Margaret Mead

I volunteered for Airborne training not because I was attracted to the idea of jumping from an airplane, but because of clear signals from the Washington Office of Personnel Management that being Airborne qualified was—in.

Along with many of my contemporaries, I saw the wisdom of getting my ticket punched. Then, I discovered another twist: I was chosen as a pioneer in a new branch-oriented course designed to reinforce administrative and operational skills. My own Artillery branch had concluded that, because of ever-advancing technological developments such as surface-launched missiles, we needed a new kind of comprehensive intermediate-level course for officers. The Field Artillery named its curriculum Field Artillery Surface to Surface Missile Battery Officers Course, then promptly reduced that mouthful to FASSMBOC. I was assigned to five weeks of Jump School followed by 38 weeks of FASSMBOC.

Jump School broke down into four weeks of training and one week of actual jumps. The strategy was to use the rigorous training to eliminate anyone unable to meet the final demands of jumping. After all, leaping from a plane wearing a parachute is a highly unnatural act and the consequences of messing up the process—even once—were lethal. So, the trainers in their considerable wisdom, made those four weeks as formidable as possible.

A typical day started with an inspection in ranks. The noncommissioned officer in charge (NCOIC), along with his cadre of clones, would ceremoniously pass in front of each candidate to express dissatisfaction with the "scum" that they had to shape up. With mock woefulness, they asked themselves what they had done to deserve the impossible task of making something out of nothing. Their perceived mission was to find the chink in each candidate's armor and hammer away until his resolve had cracked, which was tantamount to abdicating his right to be identified with the Army's finest. A sense of humor and an early recognition of the method to their madness were the basic ingredients for survival.

Next came physical training that started with the Army Daily Dozen. That system dated back to World War I, when Walter Camp—better known as "the father of American football"—devised a quick, daily training regimen for the U.S. military that he described as: hands, grind, crawl, wave, hips, grate, curl, weave, head, grasp, crouch and wing. In our case, the NCOIC would liberally add extra push-ups as retribution for our ineptness at smoothly and rapidly completing the drill. And, that certainly was not the end of our exercises. A rhythmic shuffle through a prescribed 1- or 2-mile course followed. The NCOIC leading this "romp in the woods" would exhort the virtues of Airborne using point-counterpoint chanting that served the double purpose of affirming his authority while transforming contentious individuals into members of the herd. As the group shuffled down one of many trails, the instructor searched out those exhibiting any signs of weakness and implored them to quit, thereby minimizing further disgrace to his beloved Airborne. His objective could not have been clearer: drive the irresolute to throw in the towel in favor of the preferred few who demonstrated immunity to any level of intimidation.

Early in the training regimen, minimum standards had to be met in order to continue in the program. I had good cause to be concerned about one requirement in particular: five reverse pull-ups. While at West Point, I had a history of marginal performance of tasks that demanded upper-body strength. Pull-ups executed with the palms turned inward were a particular problem for me. Now, each candidate was given three chances to pass a test consisting of 10 measures of physical prowess. I failed in my

first two attempts because of difficulty with pull-ups. Because the washout
rate on the pull-up requirement usually was high, the school had installed
an apparatus, which involved a 50-pound weight and a pulley, in the break
area, so that candidates could replicate pull-ups on their own time. By
spending every minute of my precious break time on the device, I was
able to build up enough strength to pass the test on my third and last
opportunity.

The next three weeks were devoted to pre-jump drills using 34- and
250-foot towers. Fixed harnesses mounted on the 34-foot tower were
used to teach jumping techniques. Candidates would climb to the tower
platform, assume the prescribed body position, jump and free-fall a
distance equal to the length of the risers before being snared and riding the attached cable several feet into an embankment. The 250-foot
tower was the principal device teaching landing techniques. Candidates
were strapped to a fully deployed parachute and released to fall 250 feet
before making a Parachute Landing Fall (PLF) upon reaching the ground.
When properly executed, the PLF moderated the shock of landing by a
progressive curling of the torso and legs such that the force of landing
would be absorbed by the fleshiest part of the body.

The next training apparatus was the wind machine. This was a giant
blower that was used to teach the procedure for collapsing a billowing
parachute to prevent the jumper from being dragged after landing. Train-
ees would lie on their backs with feet facing the blower and the parachute
risers fully extended. The blower was then turned on to inflate the canopy
and begin the dragging process. Candidates were trained to simultaneously roll over and pull on the risers and deflate the parachute to halt
the dragging. Sandwiched in between all of the equipment training was
familiarization instruction on cargo lashing and loading, manifesting,
marshalling, and other drills ancillary to Airborne operations.

Jump week came none too soon. The previous four weeks had severely
tested the mettle of the "legs," the nickname for all non–Airborne soldiers.
Jumping would be the easy part. Those found wanting had been quietly
shipped back to their previous units or on to new assignments.

A minimum of five jumps was required to become Airborne-qualified.
The night before the first jump was a mixed bag of frivolity, thankfulness and contemplation. No one seemed fearful. All the jump-training

anecdotes we had accumulated were told and retold to build our confidence. We were, after all, the men who had made it through that grueling month. I was especially thankful that night to think that, after only five jumps, I would be heading home to see Lillian and Mark.

The next morning, there was far less talk. All had one big question in mind: What will I do when I stand in the door?

Just prior to loading the C-119 cargo aircraft for our first jump, we tried to distract ourselves by carefully checking each other's equipment—while trying to avoid eye contact, lest our anxieties were exposed. The roar of the engines and the chiding of the jumpmasters had a settling effect. As we boarded the aircraft, I felt the queasiness that always came from the peculiar aroma of engine fuel, ship paraphernalia, and combat-attired bodies.

After all were strapped in, the jumpmaster moved around the aircraft, rehearsing the sequence of events to come. He then turned about and dramatically moved to take his position just inside the open bay at the rear of the aircraft. As he stood peering out of the door, I was struck by the lack of motion and absolute silence of each jumper. When the red light came on, the jumpmaster turned to issue the jump commands.

At that moment, I and the others witnessed one of life's rare phenomena: a moment of laser focus by every individual in our group on a single individual. In that moment, the jumpmaster held absolute power over our lives. Every eye and ear was ready for the commands we knew were coming.

"Stand up!" This was it.

"Hook up!" We were risking everything.

"Check your equipment!" This is what we had signed up for and now was the time to prove we had the courage of our convictions.

"Sound off for equipment check!"

After equipment checks were completed, the jumpmaster turned to the first jumper and ordered: "Stand in the door!"

The jumper planted himself in the door while looking straight ahead. His hands were wrapped around the left and right side of the door opening with one foot on the bottom ledge and the other just to the rear of the first. If he dared look down, he would have seen the dizzying motion of the terrain rushing by and the darting shadow of the aircraft on the sandy Georgia soil.

"Go!"

A tap on the butt was supposed to accompany the command, as if confirming each jumper's decision to leap from the plane. In fact, all of this moved so fast that there was little time to contemplate any lingering fears. Each jumper was virtually pushed out through the doorway—followed almost instantly by another comrade. The jumpmaster hurtled us into the sky as quickly as we could reach the door!

I had wondered how I would handle the life-and-death decision when standing in that doorway. Instead, the truth was that I barely recall pausing at the opening. Quite suddenly, I went from standing inside the C-119—to free falling through the air. At 1,200 feet from the earth, my entire body was jolted as my parachute opened. I felt myself violently yanked to the right. I looked up to check my canopy. I was safe! It had opened! Then, I experienced the thrill of my life as I looked around to see my fellow jumpers descending alongside and the ground rapidly coming up to meet us. As I landed, I flawlessly executed a PLF, pulled in the canopy—and quickly disengaged. Exactly as I had been taught in training.

It was over! I could truly say that it was fun. I was willing to immediately reboard the aircraft for another jump.

Vehicles were parked near the Drop Zone (DZ) to pick up the jubilant jumpers. The ride back to the barracks area was charged with the euphoria of conquering the system as well as the psychological barrier of jumping out of an airplane. There were more stories to be told than listeners!

The next three jumps were uneventful. I already considered myself a veteran as I prepared for my fifth and final qualifying jump. The only difference that day seemed to be a high humidity. A heavy rain had saturated the ground and the air around us felt like a moist blanket. My C-119 took off as scheduled and began the 20-minute flight to the DZ. On cue, the red light came on followed by the command: "Stand up!"

Candidates on both sides of the aisle immediately stood awaiting the next command—except one. Jumpmasters typically have a short tolerance for the unexpected and this one was no exception.

"Judson!" the jumpmaster screamed the man's name. "Did you not hear my command!?!"

We all could see Judson repeatedly jerking forward, trying to get up but, for some reason, he could not get on his feet.

The jumpmaster was boiling. The countdown could not be delayed or the unthinkable might happen. We might overshoot the DZ. The jumpmaster stormed back, spewing expletives directly into Judson's face. Then, he propped one foot against the foot rail and grabbed Judson's shoulder harness with both hands. As he began to violently pull on Judson's shoulders, they simultaneously recognized the source of the problem. Judson had simply forgotten to release his seat belt.

The mood now switched from general apprehension over Judson's plight to controlled pandemonium as candidates broke up with laughter while the jumpmaster scrambled and cursed his way back to the rear door. Seconds before the jump would have been aborted, we began stepping into the sky as rapidly as the jumpmaster could boot us out of that aircraft.

As I felt the jarring impact of the rain-soaked soil, I attempted to repeat a perfect PLF—but in a split second I realized that the soggy soil felt much different than in previous landings. The normal PLF motion of my body was constrained by ankle-high mud! I could feel the shooting pain as my ankle bent unnaturally. I hoped it wasn't broken! Almost immediately, though, I could sense that it was a severely sprained ankle. The embarrassment over having to limp off the DZ was more painful than the injury. My greatest concern was that I might not be able to participate in the graduation ceremony. I disguised my limp as best I could and joined the other celebrants departing the DZ as we began singing Airborne victory songs.

Fortunately, the graduation ceremony involved little more than standing in formation to be recognized as new inductees into the Airborne fraternity. I was reminded of recognition day at West Point.

This time, however, rather than departing the grand ceremony for a carefree honeymoon—I was eagerly returning to my wife, who had been shouldering all the burdens of our home while I was away. As I returned to Fort Knox, I found that Lillian was, indeed, stressed and bewildered over caring for Mark and preparing for our second child. She was further alarmed when I showed up with a cast on my ankle! I quickly relieved her of that anxiety through a combination of my exuberance over the Airborne experience and a detailed account of events leading up to my injury.

Unfortunately, we had little time to recover from my absence because we had to get ready for our next move. As we packed, I tried to hide my concern over her obvious loss of weight during my five-week absence. That it had been our first separation since Mark's birth was traumatic enough, but for the first time she had been forced to endure her helplessness and frustration alone without any reassurance from me. Mark had become her obsession. In her quest for perfection, she had rejected any concession or compromise in her expectations for him.

The other emotional blow was saying farewell to Dave and Ruthie. We knew that, given the demands of the military life, we might never see them again and that compounded our own uncertainty about the future. We had become more than friends. We were brothers and sisters and confidantes—a communion of kindred spirits that had become accustomed to bearing one another's burdens. In their final moments together, Lillian and Ruthie tearfully shared their last cup of tea while I feebly tried to share some of my tales of Airborne adventures with Dave. When there was nothing more to be said, we hugged around before Dave and Ruthie started for the door. Suddenly, Ruthie whirled around, walked across the room, picked up Mark and held him close without a word for a full minute, then turned and silently followed Dave out the door.

We arrived at Fort Sill, Oklahoma, at 1700 hours on Monday, September 10, 1956, two days before my official reporting date for FASSMBOC—the 38-week, second phase of my training. One relief was a detour through Michigan, which allowed parents, friends and relatives to see Mark. Much to my amazement, Sam turned out to be the quintessential grandfather. All who knew him were captivated by his unabashed delight in his grandson. Every minute spent with Mark was precious to him. My mother was equally enamored with Mark. Neither displayed any concern over his development. They both concluded that he would blossom in his own time.

Unfortunately, Mark did not respond in kind. More often than not, he would reject their attempts at affectionate interaction by flailing his hands or tossing aside toys offered to him. He rarely smiled, made no attempt to talk, and in general was contentious toward everyone. Lillian and I had always taken great pride in our ability to take charge of our lives and overcome all adversities, so we had trouble comprehending Mark's behavior. We turned toward questioning ourselves. What had we done or failed to do that might explain Mark's irascibility? In their attempt to reassure us, family and friends told us that it probably was due to the overwhelming press of so many unfamiliar faces and places. Mom never missed an opportunity to attest to Mark's sweetness when he had been left alone with her.

Overall, we had the reassurance that Mark was a huge hit with the home folk, but the Detroit visit was typical of the emotional turbulence we felt in those days. Long valleys of depression and guilt would be followed by short stints of joy and satisfaction—followed by chasms of deferred hope. The cycle would start over, beginning with some moment like a warm smile from Mark, but that mountaintop celebration was always followed by lengthy roller-coaster dips into the valleys of despair.

We looked forward to returning to Fort Sill. Recalling our Council Heights experience, we were delighted at the prospects of living on Post and enjoying all that the Army's Artillery Center and School had to offer. Fort Sill was a beautiful Post sustained by a great tradition. This was Geronimo country. Stories abounded about the old warrior's nearly supernatural feats. Then, he had spent his last days as a prisoner there. A Geronimo museum had been established in his honor.

The Artillery's Caisson Song was the Army's best known and loved ballad. Later, the lyrics would be slightly modified, and the song was adopted as the official Army Anthem. The Artillery Hunt Club was one of a few such clubs remaining in the military. Officers and their families were permitted to keep horses and it was not uncommon to see a polo game or groups of riders roaming the countryside in full hunt regalia. Horse-drawn caissons were still used for ceremonial purposes. This was the character of Fort Sill and we were excited about being a part of it.

Our high hopes sank when we saw our assigned housing. Our quarters at 1134 Snow Road were nice enough, but lost their glitter when we discovered that all the black officers on Post lived on the same block, which we quickly came to know as The Block. We were not told in advance about this policy of segregation. It was only after we moved in that we discovered all of our welcoming neighbors, with the exception of one family, were people of color. White officers were not prohibited from living in the Snow Road "ghetto" and one family had chosen to do so. Their presence conferred a semblance of legitimacy to the racial bias. The flag of equal access was still flying at half-mast.

Our frustration with the racial barriers was minimized somewhat by a startling surprise. Much to our delight, we discovered that my cousin and her husband lived just two doors away! Seth and Delores Spelman had been assigned to Fort Sill a year earlier. Seth was a captain in the Medical Service Corps. We could not have been more pleased! I had not seen Delores since 1945 when she and her sister, Mildred, came to Detroit from Wilmington, Delaware, to spend the summer. I had known that she had subsequently married Seth after his return from an overseas assignment, but I knew nothing about where they had settled. Along with their three children—Seth Jr., Fern, and Torin—they were now senior members of the Snow Road contingent. Delores, like Ruthie, loved people. She refused to allow the routines and sorrows of the world to rain on her parade. Both Seth and Delores had magnetic personalities and their home became the focal point for all who lived on The Block. Under Delores' tutelage, Lillian quickly learned the inside scoop on Fort Sill. She was now six months pregnant and was grateful for Delores' helpful friendship. Lillian also appreciated being able to count on my return home at the same time each day!

There was no visible effect of the move on Mark. Except for occasional moments, he remained stoic and indifferent to his surroundings. Even the natural spontaneity of the Spelman children failed, for the most part, to accelerate his development. It was as if he were saying: "I know I'm not where you want me to be—but what are you going to do about it?" We were unwitting contributors to his defiance. Playtime for Mark became a time of clinical coaxing rather than a time of unbridled play between parent and child. We were so set in our focus on household stability and good order in all things—our shared ideal of harmony and decorum and propriety—that we could not comprehend how much our biases were part of the problem. Mark simply did not meet the standards that we had established for his nesting place. In fact, following our lifelong pattern, our worst fears concerning Mark were never stated. We preferred to simply disavow the truth that Mark would always need special nurturing environments. We still hoped that he would come around and fit into our vision of an orderly home.

That compounded Lillian's anxieties about our second child, due in early December. She was always a silent sufferer and normally that approach to life's challenges had been coupled with a natural resilience. Now, though, she could not block out the gnawing fear that history might repeat itself. I had to admit to myself that, although I was hesitant to voice them, I shared her anxieties.

Mark and Kym.

9

Gyroscope

Contrasting with the older system of individual replacement, Operation Gyroscope would periodically interchange entire divisions, separate regiments, or separate battalions between overseas locations and their permanent stations in the United States. As far as possible the families of married personnel would accompany them concurrently. ... The new system was expected to raise the morale of troops and their families, increase the combat effectiveness of the Army, and lower the cost of maintaining the Military Establishment.

From Operation Gyroscope, a 1957 U.S. Army report
on this new approach to troop deployment

Our family was spinning, even before I was caught up in the Army's latest concept for moving entire military families around the world.

Kym Loren Worthy was born on December 5, 1956. In stark contrast to Mark's infancy, Kym displayed a lust for life that would challenge the most gifted parents. I would later joke that Kym charged out of the chute on a dead run and never stopped! Kym doggedly resisted conformance to any kind of routine, preferring to set her own agenda. She seemed to delight in timing her demands in direct conflict with Lillian's efforts to attend to Mark's needs. Nothing was easy with Kym. After drifting off to sleep following a feeding, she would bolt awake as soon as she touched the mattress in her crib. Her robustness coupled with Mark's lethargy began to take its toll on Lillian.

Only Lillian's high tolerance for adversity enabled her to mask the turmoil she kept locked up inside. I didn't help matters. The need for us to communicate had never been greater, but that was also a stumbling block we shared. Both of us reacted to adversity by refusing to voice our fears in the hope that somehow solutions would materialize from our positive approach to life. We both assumed that silence was better than risking words that might break into the other's comfort zone.

At first, I was able to leave home each morning and focus entirely on the challenges of FASSMBOC. I was not even aware of this new plan called Gyroscope that was conceived as a way to encourage family stability in the military. Balancing my new daily course work with the challenges of supporting Lillian and the children was more than enough to consume all my waking hours. I was pleased that the FASSMBOC refresher course seemed to be an excellent introduction to emerging missile technology. My Field Artillery colleagues were eagerly awaiting these advances. In fact, we had developed an overly rosy assumption about these advances. We saw recent breakthroughs in exotic rocket fuels and electronic command-and-control systems, giving us a long-awaited quantum leap in our quest for new tactics and battlefield systems. Prior to the advent of predictable launching and guidance techniques, made possible by the budding era of electronics, there had been only limited and incremental developments in projectile throw systems. In short, we still were closer to the era of firing cannon balls than space-age missile deployment! Military engineers now envisioned dramatic new leaps in delivery systems. Indeed, most of the new advances in rocket technology our nation's leading scientists were developing were also transferable to military applications. It was now possible for the Army to consider a wide range of new weapons. One of FASSMBOC's main goals was to convince us of the many advantages of emerging technologies. We were supposed to catch the vision for a new age in Field Artillery. Initially, there was such a surge of excitement over the possibilities that by the end of the course, my classmates and I were a bit disappointed that we had only been exposed to marginal advances. The length and intensity of the FASSMBOC program built up our camaraderie and seasoned us in our Field Artillery fraternity. But, the visionary systems we heard were on the horizon were just that—still beyond our reach in the field.

This focus on exposure to new ideas and friendships was a crucial oasis for me as Lillian and I braced for more news about Mark's condition. At the recommendation of the Post psychologist who had been monitoring Mark, an appointment was made for an evaluation at the University of Oklahoma Medical Center located in Oklahoma City. The center was an easy two-hour drive. The road was flat and straight, so Lillian and I spent the entire time focused on the highlights of our experiences in recent months. We were upbeat. The Fort Sill environment was relatively pressure-free, compared with some of our earlier postings. Lillian especially enjoyed her exposure to Delores' "don't-take-life-too-seriously" philosophy. We had high hopes for the consultation in Oklahoma City.

Upon arrival at the center, our referral initially led us to Dr. Jess D. Herrmann, a consulting neurosurgeon. After a lengthy interrogation with us, the doctor examined Mark and drafted a note for Dr. Thomas at Fort Sill: "We saw and examined this little 21.5-month-old colored boy in our office today. ... There is history of slow development throughout and it is our feeling this child is generally retarded. We have arranged for him to have psychometric evaluation by Dr. Carol Spencer Sperry at the University Medical Center on January 12, 1957."

When we got a look at the doctor's report, we were profoundly discouraged. We had expected much more substance, particularly in light of our exhaustive recounting of Mark's history to Dr. Herrmann followed by what appeared to be an equally thorough examination. The report contained neither mention of possible remedial action nor any promise of improvement with time. Later, when Dr. Spencer performed her much more comprehensive psychometric evaluation, we found no sign of the reassurance we wanted. In Dr. Spencer's tests, Mark performed at the level expected for a much younger child. An IQ calculated on the basis of the Cattell Scale was 47. Even if this figure were as much as 20 points too low, Dr. Spencer concluded: "Retardation would still be indicated." She went on to write, "At best, I would expect progress to continue slowly and that the child would be able eventually to learn the practical fundamentals of education only with special schooling. Retesting at yearly intervals to check on rate of progress may be helpful in evaluating the level of development which may be eventually achieved."

We simply were not ready to accept these doctors' conclusions that Mark's condition was irreversible—but, for the first time as parents, we could not deny the painful reality of his limitations.

Dropping into the midst of our anguish over Mark's future, the news that our family was caught up in the new Gyroscope deployment system actually was a very welcome diversion. Lillian was positively overjoyed! She had long dreamed of going overseas, especially to Europe. Nothing could darken Lillian's euphoria that, this time, I was not going to vanish for weeks on end. This time, she and the children would accompany me in this new adventure in Germany.

I was relieved that the Army's new career management system for officers actually appeared to be working! I had filed my preferences with the Office of Personnel Operations and my orders directed me to report to the 2nd Armored Cavalry Regiment-Gyroscope no later than June 15, 1957. Under Gyroscope, entire units, minus their equipment, would be rotated between the Continental United States (CONUS) and Europe. Each unit's equipment and garrison facilities would remain in place. The 2nd Armored Cavalry Regiment at Fort Meade was given the mission to raise their equipment to a high state of readiness before departure— then to transport all officers, men, and their families virtually en masse to Europe. At the same time, a mirrored deployment of the 3rd Armored Cavalry Regiment from Europe would move into the Fort Meade facilities and use the equipment the 2nd Armored had left behind. Each would also assume the other's tactical mission.

The 2nd Armored Cavalry had a long and proud history and the present leadership was fiercely determined to sustain that esteemed tradition. Tanks had replaced horses, but what remained were the classic missions of the Cavalry: observing and reporting information about the enemy, screening movement of main forces, pursuing a demoralized enemy, harassing rear areas, attacking weak points, turning exposed flanks and exploiting penetrations and breakthroughs. Those missions were as pivotal as ever to success on the battlefield. Tankers retained the *élan* of cavalrymen as well as their penchant for dash and daring. They considered themselves to be the Army's chosen ones—a breed apart. Each of three squadrons of the regiment had a Howitzer Battery in addition to three Reconnaissance Troops, a Tank Troop and a Headquarters and Service Troop.

I was assigned as executive officer of Howitzer Battery of the 2d Squadron. My commanding officer was Capt. John Smith, a smart, tall, lanky Texan with a flair of his own that easily matched that of his Armor counterparts. He knew how to play the one-upmanship game and demanded and received the right to showcase the uniqueness of Artillery. In our jargon, that meant he was eager to show Artillery red at every opportunity in contrast to ever-present Cavalry yellow—distinctive colors that stretched all the way back to markings on Civil War uniforms. We became a formidable team with Smith's aggressive, hip-shooting brinksmanship and my own inclination toward a more measured, deliberate and prudent approach to challenges. The assistant executive officer was 1st Lt. Edwin Louis Hern, an ROTC graduate of Hampton Institute. In contrast to Smith's well-earned swagger, Hern was the epitome of officers who relished rank and privilege without the professional investment in building the skills that would merit such respect. He modeled spit and polish, but often came up short when discussing professional intricacies. Hern had only recently married his wife, Beverly, who came as close to the heart of old Charleston, South Carolina society as a young black girl could hope to get. At first, Lillian and Beverly could see they had little in common, but somehow, they built an odd-couple friendship. Lillian marveled at Beverly's aspirations and seemingly unencumbered lifestyle. For Beverly, successful living was all a matter of mindset. Inviting Lillian over for tea involved an elaborate display of proper place settings and service pieces, despite their obviously meager surroundings. Beverly would snip and arrange flowers, all to present the proper setting for meticulously brewed tea. Newly wed and freshly weaned from her mother's finishing school, Beverly needed exposure to Lillian's far more pragmatic approach to living. Beverly's affectations in her own home amused Lillian, but she quickly made it clear that she would not follow suit in our home. When Beverly visited, Lillian brought out artificial flowers and Melmac, a popular style of durable dishes at that time. Sometimes Lillian served guests on simple paper plates. These two very different women wound up forming such a strong friendship that Lillian asked Beverly to serve as Kym's godmother. Of course, this led to an entire theatrical display of Beverly's new role at the Episcopal church christening ceremony for Kym.

Despite all of the superficial differences, Beverly was a committed friend. She volunteered to care for Kym as Lillian pursued further possibilities for Mark, because we now were near the Walter Reed Army Medical Center. Arrangements soon were made for Mark to be evaluated at Walter Reed. Now at 27 months, the lengthy report on Mark's status was distressing. One particular section was infuriating. In a matter-of-fact way, the evaluator described Mark's "long narrow head" with a broad nose and chin as giving him "a peculiar unintelligent appearance."

"How can he say that!" I exclaimed. Lillian was equally outraged. We regarded Mark as a handsome child.

Overall, the report was gloomy, including this passage: "All one can say at this time is that there appears to be a good degree of mental and developmental retardation. What the ultimate attainment will be will only be answered in time. I think that it would be wise however, to plan on some help from the outside and that it would be extremely remarkable if this child were to attain a normal development."

That assessment angered us as well. I told Lillian, "With all the growing ahead of him, how could the doctor be so sure that Mark will not deviate from such a bleak course?"

Despite the euphoria over the looming trip to Germany, both of us knew we were drifting back toward despair. In an attempt to take constructive action, I wrote a note that I pinned to Lillian's pillow before I left the house that next morning: "For too many, all of life is divided into spans of time that would have us either rush by or stand still. Reality, however, keeps step with time's steady cadence. The flow of time produces pleasure, pain, and indifference. Do not become mired in any of these; instead, ride the crest of life's fullness found in the lessons of each."

That little note helped to refocus our attention on living each day as it unfolded. There certainly was plenty of work to fill every hour. The 2nd Armored Cavalry was in the midst of intensive preparation for our departure. Passports had to be processed for everyone who was part of this massive move. Final ship manifests had to be developed, checked and rechecked. Arrangements were made for accompanying baggage. Even though our heavy equipment would remain in place, this kind of transcontinental move involved shipping a huge list of items we would need to carry with us to Germany. Then, the Army also offered us language classes, instruction on European road and traffic signs and qualifying tests to earn an international operator permit. They helped complete administrative requirements for shipment of privately owned vehicles and coordinated immunization schedules. That was on top of the challenges of preparing our own household for such a big move.

The USS Rose was our carrier. The ship had been outfitted to accommodate all of us. I was part of the preboarding inspection party and was delighted with the accommodations. There was a nursery on board as well

as numerous activities for kids. Everything seemed to be under control—
except the weather.

On February 4, 1958, the Rose set sail bound for the port of Bremerhaven, Germany. The first day out was pleasant enough. The cabins were
small but well appointed. The dining area was more luxurious than
expected and the food and service were excellent. Despite the bite in the
air, there was ample opportunity for strolling or lounging on the deck. I
was not too thrilled about the troop quarters but appreciated the efforts
that had been made to make them as comfortable as possible. All in all, it
was an auspicious start.

Unfortunately, the serenity of the first day was short-lived. Suddenly,
the Atlantic became more contrary than usual, even for February. Unse-
cured items became sliding missiles. Cabin doors became difficult to
open—or were hazards to passersby. The deck became untenable. Under
the circumstances, meals continued to be prepared and served as usual, but
they were sparsely attended. Lillian was one of the first casualties. She was
doubly disappointed because she had hoped to relish each day of freedom
aboard the Rose without her usual long list of household chores. Lillian
reached a point where she could barely rise up from her bed. I managed to
operate at about 70 percent efficiency. My personal discomfort was somewhat ameliorated by my preoccupation with easing Lillian's agony. The
children, especially Kym, were delighted. They thought that running to
and fro and side to side in their quest to maintain their balance was great
fun! The nights brought no relief. The giant waves caused the ship to pitch
violently—immediately followed by a leeward yaw before recovering to
pitch again. The rails of the bunks acted as bumpers for the occupants who
alternated between near standing on their heads to involuntarily rolling
over while simultaneously shifting their weight to their feet. Sleep fluctu-
ated between fitful to none at all. So intense was Lillian's suffering that the
children's sleeping through the nights provided no consolation.

The violent weather persisted throughout the remainder of the voyage.
On February 13, the Rose docked at Bremerhaven. The old concrete-and-
steel port was the most beautiful sight Lillian had ever seen. Bremerhaven
meant that her nine-day torture on the Rose was over.

Trains were ready in anticipation of our arrival. Space on each train had
been strictly allocated in order to maintain unit integrity. Soldiers traveled

with their families but maintained themselves and their accompanying equipment in a combat-ready status.

The trip from Bremerhaven to the small Bavarian city of Bamberg, which was to be the headquarters of the 2nd Squadron of the 2nd Armored Cavalry, was a scenic delight. Lillian marveled at the dozens of spotlessly clean villages, each appearing to be quainter than the preceding one. Bikers were everywhere despite the bitter cold and treacherous cobblestone streets. Historic old churches, cathedrals and an occasional castle nestled in the surrounding hills proclaimed the charm and mythos of the Rhineland. Volkswagens and small diesel-powered Mercedes snaked their way along the narrow village byways.

Despite the breathtaking beauty, Lillian soon drifted off into her first uninterrupted sleep in nine days. I played games with the children until they too succumbed to the hypnotic trundle of the train.

10

Challenges of a Cold War Command

The Soviets continue to concentrate on the development of war-making weapons and supporting industries. This, as well as their political attitude in all international affairs, serves to warn us that Soviet expansionist aims have not changed. ... Eternal vigilance and increased free world military power, backed by our combined economic and spiritual strength, provide the only answer to this threat.

President Dwight D. Eisenhower in an address to the nation in November 1957

"Next stop, Bamberg!" the conductor crisply announced. This was a wake-up call to the many men, women and children who had fallen into a much-needed deep sleep.

Because of the new Gyroscope vision of soldiers and family members moving in unison, we faced a strange and divergent path at the train station. Those of us with spouses and children were naturally concerned for their well-being—but we also were tasked with exiting that train in combat-ready status. On the one hand, I was benefitting from Gyroscope and the Army's new post-World War II focus on retaining experienced officers by caring in a new way for our dependents. On the other hand, I was an officer disembarking near the front lines of the Cold War in a high-anxiety season of fear after the Soviet launch of the Sputnik 1 satellite on October 4, 1957. The idea that the Soviets now controlled outer space was terrifying to many Americans and awe-inspiring to others. The Sputnik crisis, as that era was soon called in political shorthand, touched off both the Space Race and the creation of NASA. Before we left for Europe, President Eisenhower had addressed Americans across all radio and TV networks and, in the middle of his assessment of the high stakes we faced, he pointed directly toward my branch. He said, "Many of the traditional functions of the Army's artillery and support aircraft have been taken over by guided missiles. For example, we have already produced, in various distance ranges, hundreds of Matador, Honest John and Corporal missiles. To give you some idea of what this means in terms of explosive power: four battalions of Corporal missiles alone are equivalent in fire power to all the artillery used in World War II."

I stepped down off that train into Bamberg, Germany, as a husband and father of a family with special needs. At the same time, I stepped into Bamberg as an officer in the Cold War, going toe to toe with the Communists on this rapidly escalating playing field. I had left Lillian in her part of the train to bundle up the children in their coats, gather up their bags and prepare for our new life as a family. My focus was the troops bundling up bedrolls, steel helmets and weapons. The troops were given first priority to take the platform and form up in front of a designated member of the advance party. We could see the vehicles standing by to transport us to the post. After an inspection in rank by the squadron commander, the troops marched to their assigned vehicles and prepared to move out on a field exercise designed to familiarize us with our tactical mission and area of operations. The members of the advance party remained behind on the station platform to aid the second wave—our families.

Lillian and the other wives tried to conceal their apprehension as they watched the men pull out, leaving them in a strange land with only the promise of shelter and substance of unknown sufficiency. It was the responsibility of the squadron executive officer to provide for the needs of families until the return of the troops from the field. Buses were used to transport wives and children to what we called the *kasern*, the German word for barracks that we used to describe our neighborhood on the post for the next three years. Naturally, as the buses were loaded, members of the squadron staff were peppered with questions about the quality of the family quarters. Responses ranged from a silent thumbs-down motion to an enthusiastic, "Outstanding!"

Lillian braced herself for the worst, then found herself immediately impressed when she arrived at the *kasern* and got a look at the manicured landscaping and spacious courtyards. She liked the low, distinctive look of the architecture. These weren't typical American high rises she had seen before. Each unit was two or three levels and the style varied enough to give the place a pleasant, welcoming feel. Lillian's bus stopped at a six-family unit on *Birkenallee Strasse*.

So far, everything looked promising, but Lillian once again felt a rising anxiety. What would she find inside? Before exiting the bus, each wife was given her quarters assignment and told that her husband's name would be taped to the door. They were also told that the buses would return in two hours to take them to the commissary and PX so that they could purchase whatever was required to meet their immediate needs. Additional information detailing Post services, bus routes and schedules, medical facilities, and orientation meetings would be found in the quarters. They were also given a number to dial in the event of an emergency. A complete telephone directory would be delivered in 48 hours.

Advance-party enlisted men delivered tagged hand baggage to each apartment and assisted with the children. To say that Lillian was delighted with our apartment is an understatement. The richly paneled parlor—complete with chandelier and adjoining powder room—led into a large, well-equipped kitchen on the right. Straight ahead was a large combined living and dining area. Glass-enclosed shelving with wood trim and heavy brass-handled drawers were built into the wall separating the dining area from the kitchen. The dining table and chairs were solid walnut and comfortably seated 10 people when extended. The shelves and drawers were stocked with a complete sterling silver coffee service, flatware, and ancillary service pieces. Bavarian leaded crystal including water, wine, and champagne glasses were appropriately displayed beside the Rothenberg china service for 12. The living room area was furnished with a sofa, two easy chairs, a beautifully finished walnut coffee table, and tastefully selected accessories.

There were two large bedrooms, each with solid hardwood wainscoting and built-in shelving lining the entire length of one wall. A large bathroom with shower separated the two bedrooms. Freshly finished hardwood floors extended throughout the apartment. All beds were dressed with large feather pillows and heavy wool blankets. Extra sheets and blankets were stored in closets in both bedrooms. Lillian duly noted that all rooms and contents were spotlessly clean.

Lillian was barely able to contain her exuberance at such a heavenly haven, especially after the agonies of our transatlantic crossing. She sat down right away and prepared her first shopping list, eager to cook up a special meal for that first memorable evening as a family in our new home.

She received no word that I would be unable to reach our new home for three days.

While Lillian was taken to our new home, our 2nd Squadron moved quickly to an assembly area where we were briefed for the first time about occupying our piece of the pie we were responsible for covering. Back at Fort Meade, we thought that we were thoroughly planning for our border surveillance mission using both map and field exercises. We referred to that as "war gaming" the mission. Now, our boots were on the ground in the real world within marching distance of what Winston Churchill had called the Iron Curtain. When World War II ended, the Allies carved up Germany in what rapidly turned into an uneasy confrontation between the Soviet Union and the Western Allies, most famously in Berlin itself. When we arrived, global forces still were squaring off and jockeying for what they thought would be their final positions. The lines had not yet hardened. The infamous Berlin Wall would not be built until 1961. The stakes were still escalating all across Central Europe. As we took up our positions in 1958, the area covered by today's Germany was a complex color-coded map of occupation, including the small, specific zones within Berlin. This ratcheting up of both arms and anxieties was not what American leaders had expected in the post-WWII world. Many American leaders had hoped Germany would settle into some kind of a stable new borderland in the heart of Europe. However, the Korean Conflict in the early 1950s became a horrific warning that proxy wars could suddenly break out in this volatile new era of East-West brinksmanship. So, by the mid 1950s, the Allies were fully committed to beefing up troop strength in areas of the globe where Communist aggressors could come pouring across a border at any moment. Especially in Germany, the post-WWII occupation zones were strengthened considerably after Korea. The Allies faced a real dilemma. They were not eager to encourage West Germany to build a powerful new military force less than a decade after the Nazis has been defeated. Instead, international responsibility for defense divided the German territory into quarters. To the northeast, Soviets already controlled what we commonly called East Germany. Across from that region, covering the northwest area of the German homeland, was the British zone of occupation. The southwest region was French. American forces were tasked with shoring up the large southeast area. The focal point of our 2nd Squadron operations was the small border town of Coburg. Only barbed wire and a narrow, plowed strip of soil separated Coburg from East Germany.

Adding to our anxieties were a series of small discoveries, including the poor quality of the maps we were issued. These charts contained far less topographical detail than the textbook cartographs we were accustomed to using at Fort Meade. Except for the clearly defined autobahns, there was little to distinguish major roads from wagon trails. Critical landmarks and other essential data were almost non-existent. Finally reaching the border with East Germany, however, we could sense right away that this was a deadly serious assignment. The strip of land was kept freshly tilled by the East Germans to aid in detecting foot or vehicular movement. Coburg was the site of several towers, which were a part of a network of observation posts that fringed the plowed strip along the entire border between East and West Germany. It would also be home base for the 2nd Squadron's reconnaissance troops for surveillance of our assigned turf. One of the 2nd Squadron's three reconnaissance troop units, supported by the necessary logistical elements, would be stationed at Coburg at all times. Their mission was to report any unusual activity, including inadvertent as well as deliberate border violations. They were fully armed to protect themselves in the event of hostile activity. Together with other squadrons arrayed along that border, they were the eyes and ears of 7th Army. We all were aware that the defense of Western Europe by NATO could depend on how well our recon troops did their job.

The cavalry regiments were the vanguard and buffer for all of NATO forces in the event of an attack. Top Secret General Alert contingency plans provided the framework for a coordinated delaying action on the part of contact forces until NATO could counterattack at the time and place of our choosing. The howitzer batteries would move and deploy as necessary to provide fire support for the delaying recon and armored forces. I felt the considerable weight of this frontline responsibility. Our

2nd Squadron's first three days in the country were a crash course on the mission we had accepted.

Day One was a laborious process of making ourselves ready for our new roles. We had to inspect and sign for our equipment as allocated by the Table of Organization and Equipment (TO&E). Our advance party had already done a lot of the logistical work on these inventories and contacted U.S. Army Europe (USAREUR) Logistics Command responsible for support of our mission. Accounts were opened, then various levels of supply points were allotted for various classes of supplies we might need. Basic loads of ammunition, petroleum products and food staples had been pre-stocked. This enormous organizational challenge consumed that first day.

On Day Two, after a hot breakfast, all of D Troop and the command elements for the rest of the squadron moved out on a shakedown cross-country march, with Coburg as the terminal point. All movements had to be executed with great caution. The entire exercise would be carefully monitored by no less than USAREUR headquarters to preclude any activity that could be interpreted as provocative by East German border forces. Converging on Coburg was particularly sensitive because we were relieving temporary forces and were getting ready to begin our rotations of the three reconnaissance troops that would remain onsite for 30 days. Under the oversight of veterans in this area, D Troop would rehearse surveillance procedures and then surreptitiously assume responsibility for border security.

On Day Three, all except D Troop and necessary support elements began the trek back to Bamberg. Howitzer Battery officers and non-commissioned officers seized this opportunity to identify and chart topographical benchmarks and survey control points vital to accurate fire direction and target acquisition. We reconnoitered potential firing battery sites and observation posts that afforded the greatest opportunity for effective support of retreating armored reconnaissance forces. It was the first real opportunity for Capt. Smith and me to observe and evaluate Lt. Hern and two officers newly assigned to Howitzer Battery. Both 1st Lt. Bill Mack and 1st Lt. Tom Zetterstrom had reported just prior to movement to Germany. Mack was a quietly assertive New Englander who did what he was told but always seemed to be masking an otherwise headstrong nature. Zetterstrom was from a small town in New York. He was inclined to be a loner who had something to prove. He was bright enough but tended to be a free spirit.

As expected, we made rookie mistakes. But by force of personality, Capt. Smith was able to begin the process of binding the wounds of mishandled assignments while he built up our sense of teamwork and self-confidence. At 1800 hours on Day Three, our 2nd Squadron minus D Troop rolled into the motor pool of the Bamberg *kasern*. We had successfully silenced many concerns about our ability to get into this new game—and we all looked forward to rejoining our families.

In the meantime, Lillian had reconnoitered and started her own consolidation of her position at No. 14 *Birkenallee* A-2. Almost immediately, a new neighbor had called. Florence Sullivan was the bubbly Italian wife of Lt. Dan Sullivan who was assigned to Headquarters Troop. Florence was absolutely squeaky in her excitement about living at Bamberg. This was her first home away from Buffalo and her expectations had been low, so her enjoyment of the accommodations kept soaring as she surveyed one detail after another. Each exclamation about the virtues of her apartment was punctuated with a high-pitched, "I wish my mom could see this!" Of course, their apartment was identical to our own.

Florence joined Lillian on their first trip to the commissary and Post Exchange. Both were impressed with the service and the quality of the European-made merchandise. Neither was overwhelmed by the variety found in the commissary, particularly of fresh fruits and vegetables. For both, that shopping trip would be the first of many adventures looking into Army and Air Force exchanges all over Germany searching for bargains and little pieces of Europe to take back to the U.S.

Household goods and other baggage not hand carried were delivered on the second day after arrival. Lillian had spent the night super-cleaning shelves and mentally organizing storage areas. She and Florence had also assisted each other in rearranging furniture to their liking. Locally recruited engineers arrived to hook up washing machines, dryers and dishwashers and provide instructions in the use of transformers needed for 110-volt equipment to mate with 220-volt power sources.

Whenever I returned, Lillian was determined that we would make this new place our home, so she strategically placed favorite knickknacks around the rooms. She also had found all the ingredients for lasagna, a family favorite. After the physical challenges of the USS Rose—which involved a bland diet if any food could be consumed at all—she longed for a meal that would revive her taste buds. Fresh selections of German garlic bread and pastries would round out our first family dinner together in this new residence. She even brought out the crystal and lit candles for my return.

However, it was almost 2100 hours before I was free to go home that night. After returning from Coburg, vehicles had to be fueled, washed and parked. I also had to accompany Capt. Smith on an inspection and assessment of the readiness of the barracks to receive the troops. Then, we needed a brief conference with the first sergeant and platoon sergeants on the next day's schedule. Well past a normal dinner time, I finally began to look for our new quarters.

As soon as I sounded the heavy brass knocker, I could hear Lillian sprinting toward the door. She jumped into my arms even before I could step inside. After we silently embraced, Lillian led me into the parlor and invited me to take a good look at the new fixtures of hardwood, glass and crystal. After she was sure that I was pleased too, Lillian finally burst into a stream of acclamations—shouting her delight to the point that I wondered if our neighbors might come running. It was a moment of fulfillment—a milestone of accomplishment and a foretaste of the good fruits we assumed would inevitably continue to accrue after all of our hard work. The children already were asleep. The candlelight dinner provided just the right atmosphere for this high-spirited evening of relief and optimism. Echoing the promises from Scripture, I thought: This is what it must be like for the hind's feet to be firmly planted on high places. Nothing could dim our hopes for a glorious future.

That's when we were jolted back to reality by a whimper from Mark. Suddenly, that reminder blew an ominous wind across our imaginary horizon line. In unison, we made emotional pivots back toward our common anxieties. How had our move halfway around the world already affected Mark? Had we made the right decisions as parents? What lay ahead for our family? The transformation in our view of the world was absolutely startling that night.

The next day, as we had feared, Lillian found herself grappling unsuccessfully with one of Mark's contrary episodes. When she heard a knock at the door, Lillian yanked it open with body language that made it clear that any visitor, at that moment, was an unwanted intruder. Then, she got a good look at the small, shabbily dressed young woman uneasily wavering at the threshold. Lillian's demeanor quickly softened, then she was embarrassed as the visitor took a good look at Mark's cereal bowl and its contents splattered across the kitchen floor. The visitor grinned. Lillian was not amused, but maintained her composure.

That is how Hedi came into our lives. She was pale. We thought of her as chalky white, an impression enhanced by her red hair. She was 24 years old, 90 pounds and had a habit of speaking and smiling at the same time. Lillian got one look at her chipped fingernails and toughened hands and knew this woman was used to hard work. The fact that she spoke surprisingly good English—despite the fact that she had not finished high school—spoke well of the German schools.

As she handed papers to Lillian for inspection, she said, "I wish to work for you. My work is good. You have nice place. I must take good care."

Lillian's first reaction was disbelief. She thought this had to be some kind of mistake. Surely, Hedi had been misdirected. We could never afford a maid. Perhaps she was supposed to apply for work at the senior officers' quarters. But as Lillian reviewed Hedi's papers, which served the dual purpose of authorizing her visit as well as confirming her trustworthiness, Lillian warmed to the idea. Most astonishing was the rate: Only $30 per month for a full-time, live-in maid.

Lillian tried to conceal her excitement as she and Hedi continued to get acquainted over a cup of tea. They parted with the understanding that Lillian would contact Hedi the next day after consultation with me. Of course, I was thrilled at the prospect of help and companionship for Lillian. I urged her to complete all administrative requirements and hire Hedi as soon as possible. I was sure that if we didn't, someone else would. We were not aware that the same scenario was being played out throughout the squadron by other aspiring maids.

Hedi proved to be a wise investment. She was a model of focus and efficiency. With Hedi, there was no lost motion. Typically, she would come down from her quarters at 0700 hours, round up the dirty clothes, take them downstairs to the laundry room and sort and load the first batch. She would then return to the apartment, take off her shoes, and begin to clean the stove and refrigerator or polish the floors, depending upon Lillian's plans for the kitchen. While the wax was drying, she would either polish the silver, shake the throw rugs or clean the cupboards whether they needed it or not. In between, she would return to the basement for the next wash cycle and begin drying the previous load. The bedrooms and bath would be cleaned when available without any interruption in our routine. During unavoidable gaps in her cleaning scheme, she would bundle up the kids and take them outside for a walk or romp in the snow.

This protocol was established without any prompting on the part of Lillian. It soon became clear that Hedi only tolerated Lillian's offers of breaks in her day for a bit of relaxation and casual conversation. Hedi preferred to keep working and did not seem to enjoy such chitchat. So, Lillian eventually learned to accept Hedi's work ethic and coveted those occasional moments when Hedi encouraged personal interaction.

The children loved Hedi. She made no special effort to ingratiate herself with them and gained their favor in part by merely spending time with them when she had no other work to do. She related well to Mark because she simply saw him as a child who required special care. She regarded childcare as just another part of her daily schedule and Mark's extraordinary needs came with the territory. Unwittingly, she sometimes became the pressure relief valve that brought leverage to our emotional, and not always reasonable, reaction to Mark's irrational behavior. Best of all in this regard, Hedi never allowed her love for the children to contravene her primary obligation to us.

At home, we all were sorting out these new roles—and I was grappling with the same challenge in my new posting. As the second squadron settled into its Bamberg Garrison routine, Capt. Smith lost no time in trying to establish the identity of Howitzer Battery. He exploited every opportunity to dramatize the uniqueness of Field Artillery vis-à-vis the Cavalry. His spirited advocacy of Artillery was a source of irritation to his Armor colleagues, but was indulged, if not encouraged, by his superiors. Smith's aggressive flaunting of artillery was very popular with his troops—a morale booster he milked to the limit. One day, he actually ordered half of the façade near the barracks our men shared with Tank

Troop to be painted a bright Artillery red. No one could miss the fact that we were there in force!

Thanks to Smith's flamboyant leadership and our training skills and technical expertise, "How" Battery was quickly established as a "can-do" outfit. Despite a USAREUR-wide austere training regimen to conserve fuel and ammunition, How Battery was frequently asked to road-march to Grafenwohr, Germany, one of three USAREUR-managed major training areas, for the purpose of providing fire support for tactical units and forward observer training for troops stationed throughout the Corps area. The battery would occupy positions that enabled the M52 (105 mm) howitzers to place fire on targets in support of maneuvering infantry and armored forces as well as separate logistical elements, whose officers were required to qualify as forward observers. These forays were excellent training exercises for How Battery and were welcomed by the troops, who preferred the live fire opportunities over the "busy work" of garrison duty.

These exercises also were confidence-builders. How Battery's contribution to the border mission was limited to occasionally providing augmentation personnel to meet unusual requirements of the reconnaissance troop on duty at Coburg. These trips to Grafenwohr were the only opportunities for any realistic war gaming except for annual field training exercises. Capt. Smith made the most of each of these assignments that laid the foundation for the battery's exemplary performance during his command and beyond.

On the home front, Hedi's presence gave Lillian time to explore all of the resources available within USAREUR for special children. The professional medical contingent in Bamberg consisted of the squadron surgeon, two nurses, two contract German physicians, a dentist, and a third contract nurse. The TO&E also provided for additional medical personnel, including triage-trained men, and equipment required for our squadron's size and mission. All were housed in a combination aid station and minimum-level hospital. Coburg border operations required the presence of one of the German physicians at all times. Psychiatrists, psychologists, and social workers were posted at major Corps and Army headquarters throughout USAREUR.

After tracking her way through these complex medical systems, Lillian was referred to a psychiatrist at the U.S. Army Hospital in Heidelberg. At

0600 hours on June 2, Lillian, Mark and I set out to visit this specialist. I could see that Lillian was a bit deflated when Kym hardly blinked at being left behind with Hedi. To add insult to injury, Mark began to cry as he was led away for this road trip.

As we drove, Lillian tried to brush aside her anxiety. She could not shake the feeling that disappointment was inevitable. She dreaded the prospect of once more having to review for a doctor all the details of Mark's medical portfolio. Her despondency persisted despite my efforts to accentuate the positive aspects of our journey.

As we neared Heidelberg, Lillian began to warm up to our imminent visit. That was partly due to our discovery that we were driving into what was arguably the cultural center of West Germany. Her crash course on Germany had taught her that Heidelberg was the home of the oldest university in Germany and that the venerable Heidelberg Castle was one of the great historic landmarks in all of Europe. Situated in the tree-laced hills overlooking the Neckar River, Heidelberg was a magnificent microcosm of old Europe preserved for the enjoyment of hundreds of thousands of visitors each year.

We found that the medical facilities at USAREUR Headquarters offered a quality of services that were perhaps unequaled in any other military installation outside of the continental U.S. and Hawaii. Knowing that in all likelihood this would be the ultimate in professional staff available in Germany actually added to our anxiety concerning Mark's future, should this consultation prove to be a washout.

We were warmly received but efficiently whisked from one information-gathering station to another until all necessary interviews and forms had been completed. Then, we were ushered into the office of the doctor who was the principal assistant to the USAREUR psychiatrist. He was a no-nonsense practitioner eager to solve problems. He had little patience with his colleagues who held couch klatches, coddled and played what he viewed as mind games with their patients.

He immediately instructed, "Tell me about your son."

I began to brief him on Mark's development even as I could see him flipping open and reviewing Mark's file himself. After a few minutes, the doctor looked up and began to study me, Lillian, and Mark—as if defining in his own mind the link between the three of us. Then, he asked lots of questions. Lillian's habit of prompting me or amplifying my answers seemed of particular interest to him.

He asked, "Why did you come to see me?"

Lillian and I were taken aback. Wasn't it obvious? We had come because we needed help. Why would he ask such a question? We did not immediately grasp the significance of his query. Ultimately, he was looking for ways that our individual responses might reveal something important about our perceptions of Mark.

More questions followed: "Had we accepted the reality of Mark's infirmity? Or, were we seeking help in coping with his disability?"

I began to respond and, apparently, I was confirming everything this doctor already was anticipating about the situation. He said, "Without testing, I see no basis for any opinions contrary to those offered in Mark's file. It is quite apparent that his development lags behind the norm for his age. I am not optimistic that there will be any dramatic movement. I am not aware of any proactive or remedial initiative that we can take at this time. We will want to join with you in monitoring his progress."

Now, his message was crystal clear. The doctor was slamming the door in the face of any hope of reversing Mark's journey. Lillian was shattered. Tears welled up, just short of overflowing. The constriction in her throat would not allow her to cry aloud. The pain from the knot in her stomach was almost unbearable.

The phone rang, and the doctor excused himself with a promise to return in a few minutes.

His departure opened Lillian's flood gates. Release came in the form of great sobs. Holding her close, I made no attempt to quench the outpouring of her agony. Instead, I encouraged her to let loose the hurt and anguish born out of confusion, disappointment and guilt.

When the doctor returned, we had regained our composure sufficiently to ask our questions concerning Mark and Kym. Lillian asked: "Doctor, there are times when Mark's tantrums are more than I can handle. No amount of coaxing helps. Even spanking doesn't work. What should I do?"

Almost casually the doctor replied, "Let him do whatever he wants to do. Don't try to restrain him. Let him act it out."

Lillian and I stared incredulously. Did he mean that there should be no attempts to discipline him? No way would we buy into that piece of advice.

After that kind of counseling, the rest of the session seemed meaningless to us. The lines of communication had been severed. After the exchange of parting pleasantries and platitudes, we departed. We felt defeated. There would be no future appointments. We struggled to find any redeeming value in the experience.

As we drove back to our apartment, we could not even appreciate the wisdom of the doctor's advice. That realization came much later. Already we were focused on Christmas, which was coming soon. Lillian and Florence had made the rounds of all the nearby Post Exchanges, including the ones at Bamberg, Nuremberg and Wurzburg. They had also covered the local department stores and shops. Never before had either of them been exposed to such uncommon and intriguing curios: Black Forest cuckoo clocks, Belgian linen, Danish teak accessories, Italian marble, English woolens, Irish crystal, French leather goods—and many other delights— were in abundance.

In the process, Lillian had searched out unusual and instructive toys for the children. She still clung to the grand notion that excellence should reign above all else. There should be no time nor space for the mundane. Children should cut their teeth on that which is best and that which is lasting. Lillian wanted, more than anything else, that first Christmas at 14 *Birkenallee* to be perfect. Christmas was a celebration of the newborn Christ. In her mind, December 25, 1958, would also signal the new beginning for the Worthy family. She made festive apparel for the children, including red-and-white stocking caps and elf-style shoe socks. Tinsel was hung on the tree one strand at a time until each branch resembled a glistening formation of icicles. Decorations were tastefully displayed with all the deliberation of a professionally designed exhibition. Cookies were baked and tinned. Christmas music filled the house from dinner to bedtime each night. On Christmas Eve, we spent most of the night wrapping gifts, eating cookies, and playing Santa Claus.

Kym awakened Christmas morning only two hours after Lillian and I had gone to bed, shouting, "Mommy, Mommy, has Santa Claus come?"

She was bouncing up and down as Lillian sleepily eased out of bed. I resisted Kym's demands for a few seconds until guilt claimed me. Mark was awake but gave no indication that he was aware of the significance of the occasion. As soon as she was lifted over her bed rail, Kym squirmed out of Lillian's grasp and dashed into the living room. Lillian yelled for her to return—but too late. Picking up the Christmas outfit that she had made for Kym, Lillian soon whisked Kym away from her discovered treasures in order to properly adorn her for the occasion. Concurrently, I was failing in my attempt to get Mark to realize that he was supposed to be excited on Christmas morning. As I was ushering Mark into the living room and Lillian was frantically trying to dress Kym, Hedi arrived. She had been part of all that had transpired up to Christmas Eve. Now she marveled at the display of toys and gifts under the tree. Next, she noted Kym's crying, Lillian's frustration, and Mark's indifference to it all. She probably wondered: How could there be such sadness in the midst of such abundance?

Since the children and the tree had now been properly trimmed, it was picture-taking time. We managed to snap some shots of ourselves with a sniffling bright red-and-green-clad 2-year-old and her apathetic brother surrounded by jollily wrapped gifts and toys. Finally, the children were released to explore their toys on their own terms. But by this time, much of the excitement and spontaneity had dissipated. Undaunted, Lillian continued to create the set and props for the production of the Christmas joy she hoped all of us could experience.

Because of her natural resilience, and with the assistance of some subtle nudging by Hedi, Kym soon began to frolic amongst the boxes, bounding from one toy to another in search of a favorite, with Mark following her lead.

While I was the proud, if exhausted, father for the first major holiday that season—New Year's Eve found me on duty as the squadron duty officer. As such, I was the squadron commander's representative and the initial point of contact for any unusual incidents occurring on Wednesday, December 31, 1958 and Thursday, January 1, 1959. I was the keeper of the keys and the recipient of reports of any border activity from the reconnaissance troop on duty at Coburg. I would also make periodic communication checks with Corps Headquarters. At least twice on each of my duty days, I would physically check the posted guards to confirm their familiarity with their assigned area, their dress and proper demeanor, their knowledge of the day's sign and countersign, and their comprehension of the General Orders.

This was the first of three consecutive years that I volunteered for New Year's Eve duty in order to receive credit for two weekend duties. Neither Lillian nor I cared much for New Year's revelry, so the extra credit for weekend duty was a bonus involving a minimum of sacrifice.

The biggest milestone in mid-January was the publication of the promotions list. Nearly 10 years had passed since Capt. Smith had pinned on his tracks. I had often heard him commiserate with colleagues about how long he had been stuck at that grade. The truth was that promotion from captain to major was a big step and he knew that. So, it was a bittersweet surprise that his name appeared on the new list. One thing was certain: It was party time. Capt. Smith pooled his resources with another promoted officer and together they planned to throw a never-to-be-forgotten blowout that would showcase both the dash of the Armor and the splash of the Artillery.

The entire Officers Club was reserved in order to accommodate all of Bamberg Garrison's officers and their wives, as well as those who could be spared from their Coburg duty. The club was lavishly decorated with red and yellow bunting and other Artillery and Armor paraphernalia. Tank and artillery pieces were parked on either side of the canopied entrance to the Officers Club. A special menu, including 12-ounce tenderloin steaks and corn on the cob, had been prepared. Obtaining the corn had been a real accomplishment. Fresh corn rarely found its way to Germany. The German cooks were both dumbfounded and amused at the excitement created by a crop that they considered fit only to be fed to pigs.

Guests began to arrive an hour before the scheduled time. Merrymaking began outside the club as they rallied around the tank and artillery pieces. Armor officers gleefully disparaged the stubby-tubed howitzers. Artillery officers questioned the intelligence of anyone willing to entomb himself in a tank. They then strolled into the foyer en route to the bar, where they again clustered in anticipation of a night of no-holds-barred fun. The bartenders frantically organized their stations to respond to the known predispositions of their regular patrons.

Red and yellow tablecloths covered the tables with the phrase *Toujour Prêt* (Always Ready) imprinted on cardboard pyramids as centerpieces. Howitzer Battery officers had staked out a table that would provide a strategic advantage when serious Artillery versus Armor jousting began. Lt.

Mack had brought a working model of an old French cannon that actually fired when primed with miniature charges of black powder.

Lillian and I were both amused and amazed by the transformations in personality that erupted as the party moved into high gear. Several officers and their wives who we thought of as straight arrows wound up rapidly and permanently recasting their images. Smith and his Armor cohort led the assault on all barriers of rank and privilege. Rank temporarily lost its privilege. Windows of opportunity were briefly opened for junior officers to express their dissenting views on everything from banned facial hair to regimental operating procedures. Lt. Col. Miller astutely seized the opportunity to measure the true temperature of his young officers.

Excess in everything was the order of the day. Drinks were lined up and arrayed to mimic troop formations for roll call and inspection in ranks. Designated "commanders" lined up their "platoon leaders" to see who would be the first to dismiss their troops. Dismissal was complete only after all drinks had been consumed.

Toasts were proposed to the honorees, their wives, children, aunts, uncles, mothers-in-law, pets, babysitters—ad infinitum. Empty stemmed glasses were then stacked top to top and bottom to bottom in contests to achieve the highest stack before they toppled. Feeble and laughable attempts were made to catch them before they splattered on the tables.

A few of the better-endowed females were invited to celebrate by divesting themselves of their clothing piece by piece in cadence with their chug-a-lugging male partners. Most declined with teasing giggles. The few who hinted an inclination to comply were genially but firmly restrained. Although nothing shocking was exposed, this teasing led to an ever-more-rowdy atmosphere.

The crowning absurdity consisted of pouring all bottled remnants or partially consumed drinks, no matter the content, in a punch bowl. This concoction was then spiced with leftover nuts and party snacks. No remaining consumable was excluded from the mixture which was dubbed "the final potion." The challenge then was to guzzle down this "nightcap" as the final salute to the celebrants.

The evening had been a mind-boggling revelation for Lillian and me. I could not suppress a momentary compulsion to feel superior at the unrestrained misbehavior of this drunken rabble who otherwise called themselves officers and gentlemen. Mainly, I felt a certain sadness that this blowout was Capt. Smith's swan song. He would now move to Nuremberg for a brief stint at regimental headquarters before reporting to the Command and General Staff College at Fort Leavenworth, Kansas. Maj. Smith's near legendary identification with Howitzer Battery had terminated.

Nothing was as sobering that evening from my perspective than the realization that I was now in command.

The change of command was the first opportunity for a full-dress ceremony at the Bamberg *kasern* since the arrival of the 2nd Squadron. The new squadron commander, Lt. Col. J.R. Whittick, took advantage of the occasion to entertain local German officials. The mayors of Bamberg and Coburg, along with their police chiefs and other dignitaries, were invited to witness the ceremony from the reviewing stand. Politically, these were key people who needed to be stroked periodically. They were the ones who would have to be appeased in the event of troop disturbances or damage during maneuvers. Whittick was painfully aware of the less-than-auspicious history of the U.S. Army in Bamberg. Several years earlier, a local teenage girl had been brutally raped and murdered by an American soldier. Even after an extended period of healing between these communities and our armed forces, our presence in Bamberg was tenuous at best. At least for this festive day, the local authorities seemed to appreciate being our guests.

The passing of Howitzer Battery colors from Smith to me was particularly meaningful that day. During the reception following the ceremony, I suddenly became the most recognizable of all the 2nd Squadron commanders. Being the ranking black officer in a small German town would prove to be a distinct asset. What was sometimes referred to as my "uniqueness"—as well as the ease with which I embraced the local customs and social forms—drew a positive response from the local gentry. The revelation that I was a tennis player provided further entree into social circles, including access to the Bamberg Tennis Club.

Three months later, a local dignitary close to the mayor, invited me to play tennis. I could not have been more pleased. I had been concerned that I might not have an opportunity to play during my stay in Bamberg. A three-year hiatus from tennis was almost unthinkable. Directions to the club steered me through isolated avenues. The courts and clubhouse were shielded by a half-moon-shaped mound of earth with the entrance at one end and the exit at the other. Access was further monitored by a gate guard who admitted only members and their guests. After parking my car just inside the gate, I was escorted by a scantily dressed *fräulein* down a tree-lined walkway to the clubhouse. There I was met by my host.

"Welcome, Lieutenant."

"*Wie geht's*, Herr Doctor?" I replied.

The vine-covered clubhouse where we met sat atop a hill flanked by a patio containing tables with attached umbrellas. Large potted plants were liberally placed around this patio and hung from each window facing the courts. Terraced steps lined with carefully manicured ground cover led down to a wide concrete viewing area that divided the eight playing surfaces. A single sweep of the immaculately kept fence-enclosed courts revealed an equal number of male and female players all dressed in proper white attire.

"I'm impressed," I said, thinking that this was as nice a facility as I had seen anywhere.

"Would you like a drink?" my host asked.

"No, thank you."

People were beginning to notice me. Their expressions were warm and welcoming. I felt good about visiting.

"Will there be a court available soon?" I asked.

"*Sehr* soon," my host replied, mixing his German and English.

The match turned out to be one of the best that I had ever played. The pressure-free environment and the excitement over playing again after a long layoff lifted my game to a level I had rarely achieved. My host was a tenacious and wily old pro who had consistently bested most of Bamberg's top players. After the third game of the first set, other players and spectators began to desert the other courts and converged to witness the classic battle between my relative youth and the craftiness and finesse of a veteran of many seasons. Having nothing to lose and a reputation to gain, I played as if on a mission and narrowly defeated that determined but outgunned old warrior.

The crowd was delighted. I had become a minor celebrity. Afterward, I was invited to join the club's members for refreshments. We were offered various German beers, including a locally brewed smoked beer with the consistency of light syrup. These were complemented by a spread of wursts, cheeses and hard-crusted rolls and bread. I was introduced to a couple of local favorites: open-faced sandwiches of bloodwurst or lean, raw ground beef—which I respectfully declined. I did, however, thoroughly enjoy the rest of the buffet.

Before departing, I was given an honorary membership card that entitled me to unlimited playing time. I exchanged phone numbers with several players and promised to return soon. All in all, the experience had far exceeded my expectations.

Another lieutenant, who will remain nameless, arrived shortly after I assumed command of Howitzer Battery. His arrival was totally unexpected. There had been no advance notice of any kind. Squadron Personnel had not been advised that he was en route. He simply appeared. This lieutenant was the product of a politicized ROTC system that had been weakened by a small college in Louisiana. He was embarrassingly shy and incredibly naive to the point that I informally assigned Lt. Mack to babysit him. I told Mack, "Never let that guy out of your sight!"

Even the mundane elements of soldiering intimidated him. He never spoke unless spoken to. The troops quickly sensed his uneasiness and had no compassion for whatever might have sparked his misery. Openly expressed disdain for this lieutenant was held in check only by extraor- dinary counseling by me for the noncommissioned officers. I reluctantly concluded that either he was a total misfit or had the most severe case of what we sometimes called "green lieutenantitis" that I had ever seen. I rejected the urge to advise the squadron commander about his shortcom- ings. To do so would suggest that I could not fulfill my responsibilities as a leader of men. Reviewing my options, I decided against my natural inclination to "kick him in the pants" and instead chose to try a chaplain's approach to personal restoration. I began conducting daily counseling sessions under the guise of what I told him was new officer orientation. While there was no overt objection to my indulgence of the lieutenant, resentment festered among his peers. Despite all of my efforts, his self-es- teem continued to decline.

My concern heightened to the point that I decided to confide in Lt. Jim Dozier, the squadron personnel officer. Dozier advised the squadron commander, who predictably considered the new man to be a morale problem that time and leadership would solve.

Shortly thereafter, the lieutenant expressed an interest in acquiring a personal pistol. His peers considered this to be a positive sign. This was his first step in alignment with the norms of his fellow officers. Lt. Mack owned a .22-caliber automatic and suggested that the new lieutenant purchase a similar one through the local Rod and Gun Club. This seemed to improve matters. For the first time, the lieutenant exhibited a sense of confidence and resolve. I promptly commended Mack for his efforts in turning him around.

Now, in our counseling sessions, the lieutenant began to share intimate details of his background and seemed almost driven to share the history of his family. The transformation was puzzling but welcomed. It was almost as if he had been born again.

On the morning of May 18, 1959, Lt. Mack headed to the Battery HQ for a meeting and noted that the new lieutenant was not quite ready to join him. He needed to tidy up a bit, he said, lagging behind. Mack thought nothing of it until this new lieutenant failed to show up at the muster.

I was annoyed at him, but the matter was minor. I was busy. Then, at 1015, my phone rang.

Dozier, the squadron personnel officer, was on the other end. "You better get over here right away."

I immediately caught Dozier's sense of urgency and hung up without any further exchange. As I summoned my driver to take me to Dozier's office, I was bracing for a response to any number of crises. Had there been a border incident? Had a wayward man run afoul of the local police?

I was totally unprepared for what I found. Dozier minced no words. "Your lieutenant was found shot in the head by the *hausfrau* at the BOQ."

Stunned, I waited for further explanation.

"The CID is investigating. It looks like an accident. His .22 was found on the floor beside him. That's all I know."

Mumbling that I was going to the BOQ, I headed for my vehicle, telling my driver, "Take me to the BOQ."

Two staff cars were parked haphazardly at the entrance to the BOQ. Dozier had alerted the CID's team leader that I was on the way. A captain greeted me and directed me to the manager's office.

"How is he?" I asked. Dozier said he was shot but I had no idea of the severity.

"He's dead."

"What happened?"

"Preliminary findings indicate that he died from a self-inflicted .22-cal bullet wound to the temple. It could have been accidental. Cleaning equipment was found nearby. No note was found." I knew right away what had happened. The captain's tone and expression made it clear that this was no accident.

The captain was summoned to the phone. I took the opportunity to excuse myself and offered to assist in any way that I could. The meeting ended with a promise to apprise me of the results of the investigation and final disposition of the case.

I returned to my vehicle without a word. My driver, who had learned of the death from a BOQ employee, intuitively turned the vehicle toward Squadron Headquarters.

Lt. Col. Whittick was standing in Dozier's office when I entered the ante room. I solemnly reviewed my conversation with the CID.

Whittick interrupted me. "Do you think it was suicide?"

"Maybe," I said. "He didn't leave a note. He seemed to be coming out of his shell. Lt. Mack spent a lot of time with him—said that he was coming around. Two weeks ago, I decided to lean on him a little to get him motivated. We had tried everything else. But I never did lean on him, because Mack seemed to think he was over the hump."

After a round-robin of questioning stares had been exchanged, I was dismissed with instructions to contact the chaplain to initiate appropriate family notification and support procedures.

I wrote a personal note to his parents. Their response was swift and polite but enigmatic:

"Thank you for your kind and reassuring thoughts. He was a good boy who meant well even if he was a little mixed-up at times. We had hoped that the service would bring him around. I'm sure that you took good care of him and did all you could to make a man out of him." The note continued. As I read the whole text, I realized: They are not raising any questions about his death. In my note to them, I had not indicated that I thought this was a suicide, but their response to me let me know they had considered this possibility. I surmised that, to this family, the Army had been a haven of last resort. Their words expressed a pathetic but undeniable sense of relief. It was clear that the confluence of his heritage and circumstances had produced the ultimate manifestation of a troubled young man. For this young man, life in the Army had become an impenetrable jungle with no avenue of escape.

Real and Perceived Threats

Most of the major military conflicts between the end of World War II in 1945 and the collapse of the Soviet Union in 1991 were fought in Asia and the Middle East. Ironically, Europe, where no war was fought, was the epicenter of the Cold War. The stakes were highest there for both sides as two fundamentally opposed ideologies and political systems confronted each other across the so-called Iron Curtain.

Forging the Shield, a U.S. Army history of the Cold War

We have tanks too.

A Soviet commander warning Americans of the danger of the Cold War military buildup in Germany in 1961.

It was vacation time. Lillian had decided that our first European venture would be a three-day trip to Paris. She had made all of the arrangements through the Bamberg Special Services Office. The trip would include a stopover in Nancy in northeast France to visit a couple we had met while stationed at Fort Knox. He was a member of the Transportation Corps trucking company posted at Nancy. She had been a reclusive young Creole bride befriended by Lillian in an effort to ease her transition from the comfortable confines of the bayous to the ever-expanding world of the military. She had kept in touch after being transferred to Nancy and had been virtually begging us to visit them.

Lillian decided to take Kym but leave Mark with Hedi. I had convinced her that a respite from Mark would be therapeutic for both.

Nancy was located 150 kilometers west of Strasbourg near the junction of the Meurthe and Moselle rivers. There were many aesthetic incentives to tarry awhile in Nancy, but time would only permit a brief visit with our friends. After spending the night, and following a tearful goodbye, we found our way back on the road to Paris.

The great city appeared as an oasis that emerged out of the nondescript countryside. As we approached, the smoky grey structures on the horizon camouflaged the beauty that was to be found inside the walls of the city. From a distance, there was little to suggest the legendary splendor of Paris. Driving through the outer edges of the city, everything appeared to be soaked and sagging with the weight of history. With few exceptions, the building facades were irreversibly yielding to the ravages of time and benign neglect. Deterioration was everywhere. Yet there was an inescapable charm about it all.

Traffic and congestion increased exponentially as we approached the hub of the city. As we moved along the Champs-Élysées toward the circle of traffic that ringed the Arc de Triomphe, we were so intimidated by the near-lunatic driving of the French that we parked our car as soon as we could and did not drive again until we departed the city.

After we settled into our hotel, Lillian explained that she had prepared a prioritized list of places to visit in Paris. While she was tending to Kym in the bathroom, I checked this list for the first time. I was amused to see that ahead of such historic monuments as the Louvre, Montmartre, and the Eiffel Tower, was a visit to the Arc de Triomphe so that Kym could feed the pigeons.

Lillian was right! Kym stirred the favor of pigeons, Frenchmen and other tourists as she sprinkled corn kernels over the pavement surrounding the famous landmark. As I surveyed the scene, I was no longer trivializing Lillian's plan to stage what was rapidly becoming a minor spectacle. I could not suppress my pride and feverishly took photos from multiple angles for posterity. I wasn't alone! Complete strangers also were scurrying about to capture the charm of the moment. For Lillian, Kym's caper was the high point of our visit.

The Louvre was next on the agenda, followed by a trek to Montmartre. Aspiring artists were everywhere. I was intrigued by their seeming obliviousness to anyone passing by or standing beside them to observe their work. There seemed to be little effort to buy or sell. This was the Paris I had expected. Montmartre epitomized French arrogance blended into a casual sophistication found no place else. After visits to Napoleon's

Tomb, the Eiffel Tower, Notre-Dame Cathedral—and many sites along the Seine River—it was time to bid farewell to Paris.

More than anything else, this trip had been a fulfillment of Lillian's dreams. Just before our departure, I slipped away to purchase an expensive black leather bag that she had admired earlier. For Lillian, it had captured the elegance that was Paris. She would treasure it for the rest of her life.

Such was Lillian's life in that era with all the highs and lows that came with military life—from far-flung journeys together to the long and often indefinite periods as a single parent while I was away. That was our family life: sometimes united and sometimes separated. At that point, we knew all about these highs and lows.

About an hour and a half before arriving back in Bamberg, Lillian fell silent. I could feel the anxiety welling up in her—rising with each turn of the car's odometer. Kym was asleep in the back seat. The hum and slap of the tires as they met the road served as a partial diversion from a total relapse into the emotional doldrums that had intermittently plagued us since Mark's condition had been confirmed.

As our car made the turn on to *Birkenallee*, we could see Hedi and Mark playing on the open field adjacent to the building. A pervasive sense of guilt swept over Lillian as Hedi happily approached us as we exited the car. Mark made no movement toward us. His reaction was no different than if we had been perfect strangers. Lillian lifted and cradled him to her breast and asked, "Did you miss Mommy?"

Mark turned his head to look away without a sound. As I moved around Lillian, anticipating a gleeful face-to-face encounter, Mark again ignored our advances with the same nonchalance as if we had just returned from a short visit to the neighbors across the hall. Only Kym's delightful squealing as Hedi dropped to her knees to greet her rescued the moment from total disaster.

Lillian vowed she would never leave Mark again.

At 0400 the next morning, a United States Army Europe (USA-REUR) alert was called. In accordance with alert procedures, my driver picked me up 10 minutes later to take me to the prescribed assembly area for personnel and equipment checks. Subsequently, we would stand by for an unspecified time for further instructions.

At 0500 hours, Lillian was rushed to the U.S. Army Hospital/Wurz-burg-Bamberg Annex because of severe abdominal pains. She complained to the staff physician on emergency duty that she had been sick all night with an upset stomach. Finally, she admitted that she had been experiencing similar episodes for two years. She was given prescriptions to cope with the discomfort and scheduled for extensive testing. After five days of further consultation, observation and testing, she was diagnosed as having a duodenal ulcer with partial obstruction and moderate hypochromic anemia probably related to dietary deficiencies.

Why hadn't I known? A wave of guilt engulfed me. Thinking back, I should have suspected that all was not well with Lillian. I recalled changes in some of her long-standing preferences. For instance, she had stopped drinking coffee, which had been one of her favorite moments of the day. She had spent more and more time in the bathroom. Eventually, a whole series of puzzle pieces came together.

Also unbeknownst to me, another crisis was brewing on the home front. The relationship between Lillian and Hedi was beginning to deteriorate. Hedi was supposed to be our maid and nanny, but she began to assert her authority in inappropriate ways. Most likely, this was because she could see the intensity of Lillian's struggles firsthand and was overcompensating. But Hedi's assertiveness soon ran head on into Lillian's refusal to tolerate any trespassing—real or imagined—on her role as mother and head of our household. The tension rose without my noticing the looming crisis. Then, one day, Hedi quit.

I naively bought Lillian's explanation that this had been a "maid raid," a common problem in a community where lots of families were competing for the best helpers. Looking back, I regret that Lillian felt she had to construct this whole rationale around Hedi's departure. It was only later that I finally uncovered the real reason for her departure. At the time it happened, Lillian was working hard to conceal from me the depth of her daily struggles with illness, housekeeping and parenting. As Lillian woke up each morning, she was facing her own array of real and perceived threats. That is why she told me that she wanted to try to have a "normal" son.

I did not know what to say. I was emotionally ambivalent, torn between wanting to please Lillian with this new desire she was repeatedly voicing—and my love of Mark and practical acceptance of the fact that we really had all we could handle as parents. I should have known that Lillian's request, as much as it was interwoven with all the complex issues we were facing, was really a *fait acompli*. One day, as I returned from a field exercise, the children were otherwise engaged, Lillian and I had some precious time all to ourselves. And, Jennifer Elizabeth Worthy was born nine months later.

In February, 1961, Winter Shield was my last major operation in Germany. That was the name of the annual USAREUR exercise scheduled for harsh winter weather to determine the readiness of NATO forces to meet the perceived threat of Warsaw Pact nations. The bitter cold tested not only equipment performance but troop mettle, as well. Plus, by scheduling our movements when the terrain was frozen solid, we also minimized the damage caused by our heavy armored vehicles.

By this time, I had been promoted to captain and relieved of my command of Howitzer Battery. I was given the designation S-3, Plans, for the squadron. For an Artillery officer to be given responsibility for the tactical planning of an armored squadron was unprecedented and a high vote of confidence. It was now my task to develop squadron operational plans based upon the overall Winter Shield scenario to include coordination of fire support, maneuver and logistics. This was a monumental undertaking. It involved every facet of squadron operation, including preparation and movement to the exercise area, offensive and defensive battle planning. The biggest challenge was contingency planning to accommodate the capriciousness of a battle we were going to play out—surrounded by the daily lives of all of our civilian neighbors who mainly wanted us to leave them alone. The entire operation had to be adapted so that multinational forces could mesh perfectly across all the boundaries of language and culture. Winter Shield optimistically called these thorny problems "liaison and communications opportunities."

Our 2nd Armored Cavalry (2AC) was the eyes and ears of VII Corps. Spread thinly across the entire Corps front, the 2AC's mission was to find and maintain contact with the enemy and screen the movement of NATO forces. In concert with the USAREUR and Corps battle plan, I developed an operations order that detailed the squadron's role in a coordinated delaying action by NATO forces. My plan also envisioned tactics designed to lure opposing forces into killing grounds. It was also necessary to prepare alternate plans in anticipation of deviations that would be injected by exercise umpires to test unit reaction to unexpected enemy activity. As the exercise unfolded, it became painfully clear that the squadron's greatest enemy was the weather. Wild swings in atmospheric conditions had a more decided effect upon communications than did the terrain or electronic countermeasures. Bitter cold took its toll on men and equipment and sudden thaws bogged down vehicular movement and dramatically increased maneuver damage. The weather also forced other compromises in the conduct of the battle. One of the biggest was our realization that the freeze-and-thaw cycle resulted in our chewing up the environment. Local officials would not be pleased!

Nevertheless, the regiment acquitted itself admirably and was one of the few bright spots of the exercise. The 2AC emerged battered but wiser and my performance had again exceeded expectations. My reputation was assured and, perhaps, had reached the point of diminishing returns. No matter the extent of my assignment to the 2AC, there would be little opportunity for me to trump past attainments. Washington's assessment must have been likewise. Orders sending me back to Fort Sill for the Artillery Officers Career Course were awaiting my return to Bamberg.

Lillian was ambivalent about returning to the U.S. She had enjoyed our tour in Europe, particularly the first two years. In addition to the trip to Paris, we had sandwiched in a weekend excursion to the Armed Forces Recreation Center at Garmisch-Partenkirchen as well as trips to the World's Fair in Brussels and to Oberammergau for the world-renowned Passion Play. She had loved traveling the Bavarian countryside and had developed a deep affinity for the German people. She told me, "There's still so much for us to see!"

On the other side of the coin, Mark's progress left a lot to be desired and she had looked forward to returning to the States where, hopefully, things would be better for him. She fervently prayed that we would fly home. Dread of another boat ride was her worst nightmare. Going back to Fort Sill as the wife of "Captain" Worthy had a special appeal for her.

Her worst fears were dispelled when she learned that we would fly home via Military Air Transport Service on March 6, 1961.

12

New and Old Worlds

People are trapped in history—and history is trapped in them.

**James Baldwin in "Stranger in the Village," written
after his return to the U.S. from Switzerland**

*Love recognizes no barriers. It jumps hurdles, leaps fences,
penetrates walls to arrive at its destination full of hope.*

Maya Angelou

We arrived at McGuire Air Force Base in New Jersey tired but excited to stand on U.S. soil once again. Then, at the U.S. Customs counter, we were confronted by two less than hospitable agents.

First, they questioned us at length, then told us to open our luggage. I was unhappy about the casual way they pawed through our personal items. During the entire inspection procedure, the agents never looked us in the eye. Lillian could not shake the feeling that they bore an ill will. I was slower to reach that conclusion but became concerned when the men zeroed in on my SLR camera. This was a new model from Exakta, one of the oldest camera producers in Germany. These experts had been making high-end cameras since before World War I and were known around the world for the quality of their craftsmanship.

The customs agents converged over my Exakta. One asked, "Do you have papers authorizing you to bring this camera into the United States?"

"I didn't know papers were required," I said, trying my best not to convey my annoyance. I was simply telling the truth. When I invested in this camera, no one had warned me that any special import conditions would accompany it.

The officials glanced at each other—obviously gloating over their discovery.

"You have two options," the lead agent told me. "You may leave the camera with us until import authority has been confirmed. We will then ship it to you c.o.d. or we will have to remove the trademark from the face of the camera before we can release it."

"How can you do that?"

"We will use a pumice stone to grind it off."

I was crushed. The trademark was permanently imprinted in raised lettering on the body of the camera. My prized possession would forever be partially defaced and the object of questions and unspoken suspicions about how it came to be so. However, I definitely did not want to leave it for fear that I would never see it again. My anger rose. I had never heard of such a customs procedure.

In their faces, I could tell that these men delighted in their power over us.

Lillian boldly proclaimed: "We won't leave it here!"

One of the men took the camera to another room. Five minutes later, he returned. The trademark had been sloppily ground off with no regard for the resulting aesthetics of the camera. I was furious! I knew these men had intentionally taken advantage of us—for no reason other than spitefulness. We were forced to helplessly witness the violation of our property before our eyes.

I wanted to turn around and fly back to Germany.

Reigning in my fury, I managed to limit my response to sarcasm: "Welcome home to the land of liberty and justice for all!"

Buses took us, along with others, to Fort Hamilton, New York, to pick up our cars, which had preceded us on a cargo vessel. After arriving at the Post Guest House that evening, I thumbed through the Fort Hamilton telephone directory on the chance that I might find a familiar name. Suddenly, I couldn't believe my eyes. But there it was: "Maj. Seth Spelman."

I immediately dialed the number and heard Delores' familiar voice.

"Unbelievable!" I shouted into the phone and yelled for Lillian at the same time. "Unreal!"

After jubilant exchanges over the phone, I was given directions to their quarters. The reunion with the Spelmans was a welcome distraction from the pain of the customs debacle. In the Spelman household, all was well: The children had grown and Seth was obviously proud of having become a field grade officer as well as earning his Ph.D. It was a joyous occasion for all of us.

As we finally headed westward for Detroit, I savored the glow of the hospitality in their home—but I also kept replaying the incident with the customs agents, rolling the details over and over again in my mind. I wish I'd said this! I wish I'd done that! Eventually, I tried to dismiss that entire experience as beyond redemption. We were back in the U.S. again—safe and mostly sound, except for my poor camera and my wounded sense of justice.

The closer we got to Michigan, my spirits also soared in anticipation of finally being home again with our extended families. Just as I envisioned, our homecoming was a big event. Both families treated us as celebrities and contended for our time and attention. I had been given 30 days before I had to report to Fort Sill. Lillian was due in two months, so we decided she would remain in Detroit until the baby was born. Assuming I could make the arrangements at Fort Sill, I would return to Detroit after the birth and drive back to Fort Sill with Lillian and the children.

Having made our plans, we unreservedly enjoyed three straight weeks of reunions with family and old friends. Lillian's pregnancy was no hindrance to her indulging in all of the festivities. For me especially, it felt good to be back in Detroit amongst my own.

Lillian and I had been pulled into an ever-expanding new world since our wedding at West Point—but we had not lost our awareness of who we were back in that old world of Detroit's inner city. My own attitudes about living in these two worlds had evolved and expanded as well. Despite an occasional painful incident like the confrontation at U.S. Customs, I was reaching the conclusion that the richness and strength of my heritage was more of an asset than a liability. I had a solid foundation of faith and moral values. I knew who I was, and I wasn't going to be swayed by temptation to pretend that I was someone else. I knew that I was loved by God and family and friends.

That conviction was profoundly reinforced when I decided to pass through St. Louis on my way down to Fort Sill. This time, I wasn't forced to find a black motel. Lillian and I had friends in the region. Dave and Ruthie Jones insisted that I lay over with them. They had returned to their hometown of Kirkwood, a suburb of St. Louis, after completion of

Dave's military obligation. I eagerly looked forward to seeing them for the first time since our families had been constant companions at Fort Knox, Kentucky.

The 13-hour drive to St. Louis was exhausting. As I approached my destination, the challenge of finding the Jones's residence kept me alert until I pulled into their driveway. Exterior lights flashed on as Ruthie ran from the side door to meet me, closely followed by Dave and his two daughters. Ruthie grabbed me just as I emerged from my car. I shook hands with Dave while still hugging Ruthie. Stooping to greet the children, I wished Lillian could have shared this moment. She would have loved this reunion!

Ruthie had been thinking exactly the same thing. She insisted on telephoning Lillian. When they connected, Ruthie loosed a torrent of chatter and emotion. Her tears flowed unabatedly. I wondered if Lillian was responding in kind.

Dave and I drifted away while Ruthie remained temporarily oblivious to everything except her conversation with Lillian. Dave wanted to know all about my experiences in Europe. I wanted to be updated on Dave's ventures as an entrepreneur. He had taken over his father's printing business and made a few waves as he recycled some of the older employees who, over the years, had evolved into old cronies of Papa Jones. It was a highly competitive business where innovative layouts and formatting were the best insurance against loss of clients and yielded the best opportunity for growth in market share. I had only to look around to realize that Dave was more than holding his own.

The children, too, were clearly their handiwork. Both were delightfully bright, high-energy kids who looked like poster children for the emerging free-spirit movement.

Except for Lillian's conspicuous absence, the evening was uplifting by any measure. The only downside was my commitment to being on the road early the next morning. Late that night, I retired to the guest room. The canopied four-poster with a thick mattress and oversized pillows was the centerpiece, surrounded by Ruthie's original artwork. Once again, I wished Lillian had been with me. I drifted off to sleep.

Dave had already left for his shop before Ruthie rousted me for breakfast. While I was enjoying "from scratch" biscuits, Ruthie wanted to know about Mark. I shared an abbreviated version of Mark's recent history, punctuated by accounts of Lillian's recurring illnesses. Ruthie made no attempt to conceal her heartache. Deliberately, she walked around the table, stood momentarily staring at me, then impetuously sat on my lap and hugged me while swaying back and forth. In her compassion, she vicariously searched within herself for a response that would convey the depth and breadth of the hurting she felt for me, Lillian and Mark. I was deeply moved by Ruthie's empathy.

Thanks to Dave and Ruthie, the road to Fort Sill was smoother. Except for occasional tornado alerts, April was a good month to arrive at Fort Sill. The biting Oklahoma winter winds had moderated to a pleasant spring breeze. The wind and the imposing sight of Signal Mountain kindled memories of Council Heights, Medicine Bluffs and FASSMBOC. As I turned onto Fort Sill Boulevard, history seemed to reverberate throughout the bluffs and valleys so prominent within the confines of the reservation. The distant thunder of the big guns seemed to cement Fort Sill's place in antiquity for me.

The Artillery Officer Career Course did not start until July 1961. In the interim, I was assigned as a project officer in the gunnery department. This designation was intentionally flexible, and I soon wound up working with the Field Artillery Data Computer (FADAC) branch. FADAC was an experimental computer with the goal of developing faster and more accurate ways of computing firing data. Analysis of field data was underway to determine real-world viability of the system. Many skeptics saw FADAC as another attempt by Field Artillery to climb onto the wave of technology despite a questionable return on investment. It was regarded as merely the "in" thing to do. After all, opponents argued, there were no significant real-time advantages since an experienced team could manipulate manual equipment as fast as a FADAC operator could input the necessary data for electronic computation and display.

The debate ran in circles around the new equipment. FADAC supporters generally conceded parity in the speed of computation but contended that the computer was more accurate. Scoffers cited the cost and "fieldability"—the challenge of transporting and maintaining reliable equipment under all weather conditions. I came to this project with no fixed opinion. Therefore, my contribution was considered valuable by both constituencies. After a crash course on FADAC and extensive consultation with evaluation team members, I diplomatically lined up with the FADAC detractors. I concluded that FADAC had image value but offered no significant operational advantages. Indeed, there was substantial evidence that in some scenarios, FADAC lagged in responsiveness to the old manual system. That was the status of computers in that era—just too slow in real-world situations.

Other assignments, such as attending a basic electronics course and a short course on the "Little John" rocket system, consumed my remaining time before I commenced the Artillery Officers Career Course.

Jennifer Elizabeth Worthy was born on May 3, 1961, in Detroit. There were no complications. The entire pregnancy had been trouble-free. Lillian's disappointment over the baby's gender was short-lived—lasting little longer than from the time she was told that she had a new daughter until she was able to hold the baby and be reassured that all was well with her. The only downside to the blessed event was my inability to return from Fort Sill to be with her. She had prepared for my absence but was let down nevertheless.

While recuperating, Lillian had more help than she wanted. As my mother exercised what she perceived to be a grandmother's duties, unspoken tensions began to fester. Mom's intervention was innocent enough, but Mom did not understand Lillian's emotional turmoil. The Mark factor also figured into the growing clumsiness of their relationship. Mom was understandably bewildered and concerned about Mark. She was convinced that he was simply a slow starter and, in time, would blossom into a robust youngster, given enough love and patience. She suffered from an unwavering trust in conventional parenting. She believed that children, even if impaired, are predictable and, therefore, appropriate nurturing will assure continuous development. She simply could not accept that Mark's development was different—and always would be. Mom kept providing all manner of advice about what was best for Mark—while Lillian already knew what was best. These repeated conversations evolved into what Lillian regarded as nagging, then skirmishes between the two of them, and finally into full-blown acrimony.

Adding to Lillian's frustration was her annoyance that I had not been able to return for Jennifer's birth. She kept thinking that I could have returned, if only I had wanted to do so. She was not entirely wrong about that. Although it would have been quite a challenge, I could have swung a road trip to Detroit when Lillian was due. But, I had reasoned that our two families were surrounding her with all the care she could possibly need. Plus, I thought that saving our resources and then having her take a plane with the children would save them all the stress of a long, exhausting car trip. Lillian saw it as indifference. I thought I was being practical. Only later was Lillian able to fully let me know what she truly thought of my infernal logic.

In the meantime, I had secured family quarters. We were again in Artillery Village, but this time there was no area set aside for black officers. For the next nine months, we would be duplexed with Ed and Peggy Weathers and their three children: Darlene, Butch and Beverly. The Weatherses stemmed from old South gentility. Their penchant for smiling, syrupy speech, and easy-does-it manner instantly endeared them to me. Their warmth and openness was strikingly analogous to the Joneses with one glaring difference—Peggy was as laid back as Ruthie was impetuous. Ed and I bonded right away. I was certain that Lillian and Peggy would likewise come together.

I had arranged for our household goods to be delivered before Lillian arrived from Detroit. In an attempt to cushion Lillian's return to household labors, Ed, Peggy and I decided to arrange major items of furniture and other belongings. I knew we were risking Lillian's wrath by this preemptive incursion into her domain. On the other hand, there were few options for placing the furniture in 1,200 square feet of highly compartmented space. Besides, Lillian would be spared the agony of assessing whatever damage had befallen our household in transatlantic shipment. Fortunately, there was no breakage—not even a single chip in any of the china or crystal. I wished that Lillian could have witnessed Peggy's wonderment as piece after piece of our Danish teak furnishings purchased in Germany was removed from the packing crates. Since much of it had to be reassembled, Ed and I sowed the seeds of a long and enduring friendship in the process.

I arrived at the Oklahoma City Airport two hours before Lillian's flight was scheduled to arrive. As I sat in the waiting area, my eagerness to see them step off that flight was marred by a feeling of dread. I rejoiced in the realization that I was about to be reunited with Lillian after the longest separation of our marriage. I had most assuredly missed little winsome Kym. I was jubilant over the prospect of seeing Jennifer for the first time. And Mark? I was eager to see Mark, too, but I also felt all the weight of parental responsibility for Mark settling on my shoulders once again.

The announcement of the flight's arrival snapped me out of my doldrums. I positioned myself so that Lillian would spot me as soon as she emerged from the passenger tunnel. After most of the incoming passengers had filed out of the tunnel into the waiting room—there came Kym, pulling free of a flight attendant's hand.

"Daddy! Daddy!" Kym, shrieked and dashed toward me. Even after I was clearly in view, Mark's hand remained clasped in the attendant's hand. He looked at me apathetically. Lillian followed, carrying Jennifer and hand luggage. I detached myself from Kym as gently as I could and hastened to Mark. As I approached, Mark managed a flicker of a smile and slowly moved toward me at the urging of the stewardess. As we embraced, my expectations tilted from despondency to cautious optimism.

Lillian watched, expressionless, until I moved toward her. She smiled almost imperceptibly as I hugged her as best I could with Jennifer cradled between us. As we parted, Lillian thrust Jennifer toward me.

"Here's your new daughter," she said. She was shooting a clear signal of resentment in my direction. I realized that I probably should have made the effort to drive to Detroit.

I gushed over Jennifer. My love for this new daughter was flowing freely now. I glanced at Lillian to see whether her obvious annoyance was subsiding—and could tell right away that this uneasiness was not going to quickly evaporate.

On the ride to Fort Sill, Lillian remained subdued. I lamely tried to rouse some family spirit. Only Kym took the bait. Having no competition, she dominated the conversation all the way to Fort Sill. By the time we reached our carport, I had played all of my "welcome home" cards. I could only hope that the excitement of our new home and the virtues of our new neighbors would disarm Lillian's wounded spirit.

As she surveyed her new domain, Lillian struggled to maintain her cool composure. I had been hoping to see another of her joyous pirouettes. I realized I had badly misread this situation.

There was a knock at the door. I was relieved at this break in the tension. Standing at the door were Ed and Peggy with Darlene, Butch and Beverly trailing behind. Easy and earnest introductions followed. We exchanged greetings and talked warmly, standing in the entryway for a full 10 minutes before anyone made a move towards more comfortable surroundings. Peggy had brought fried chicken, macaroni and cheese, cornbread and blackberry cobbler. Right away, Peggy sensed Lillian's reserve at what I hoped would be a warm meeting of new friends. Then, Peggy sheepishly announced that the dinner was for both families. Ed immediately chimed in, explaining that they thought there was no better way to demonstrate their neighborliness than to share in a food offering. Lillian was polite but it was obvious to all of us that there was unfinished husband-and-wife business that was being deferred in light of this robust greeting.

Getting that meal organized, given the circumstances, was a testimony to the grace and ingenuity of Peggy Weathers. She delicately held sway over the entire operation without dethroning Lillian in her own kitchen. None of Lillian's dishes or serving pieces were disturbed—unless by her own hand. Another saving grace was that our children were instantly compatible. They seemed totally oblivious to the awkwardness of the adults. Even Mark had a good time that night. I think Mark appreciated that, for once, he was neither the center of attention nor the odd child out.

The dinner was a resounding success. Conviviality reigned, and a lifelong friendship was established. Lillian's spirit had risen from the ashes of despair to a far happier place. This warm welcome home had, at least temporarily, absolved me of my earlier dereliction.

In coping with the challenges of adapting to family life in yet another new home, I had the advantage of being able to walk out the door each morning and focus on the Artillery Officers Career Course. The program was divided into two phases. The first six months would be spent at Fort Sill. The class would then be placed on temporary duty to the Army Air Defense School at Fort Bliss, Texas, for the last three months. Field Artillery—consisting of both cannon artillery and surface-to-surface missile artillery—was the focus at Fort Sill. Air Defense Artillery—embodying conventional ground-to-air automatic weapons as well as ground-to-air missiles—was the focus at Fort Bliss. Approximately 20 percent of the officers selected for this course had spent their careers in Air Defense units and knew little about Field Artillery. The rest of the class was lacking in our knowledge of Air Defense Artillery. Much of the Fort Sill portion of the course had been redundant for me and the other officers who had previously attended FASSMBOC. That gave me an easy ride through the first six months of the Career Course.

Once again, Lillian shouldered the daily demands of our household, but I quickly discovered that I had more time to help in finding local resources to meet Mark's needs. Together, we searched out professionals and facilities equipped to provide growth opportunities for exceptional children. Finding no appropriate program on Post, we sought help from the Lawton school system. Our timing was perfect. The introduction of a special education class had been planned for the beginning of the school year but had been delayed because of deferred approvals for the funding. Despite the fact that the designated teacher had abruptly departed the state, school officials decided to proceed with the class and assign the job to a highly respected teacher's aide on an interim basis. This woman—with no formal special education training—had been given a classroom with instructions to set up the program and make it happen.

Lillian and I were concerned. We feared that this woman faced an impossible challenge. We were surprised that her unconventional approach proved to be highly effective. First, she invited each family individually to her home for dinner. This enabled her—and also her husband—to become acquainted with the entire family and observe their interactions firsthand. Mark's performance at the table as well as his overall level of socialization that evening was quietly noted as something to discuss later. We had never heard of a teacher doing something like this—but Lillian and I both liked this holistic approach. Lillian, in particular, was impressed with the teacher's absolute commitment and lack of pretense. A fast friendship was born as we both recognized the advantages of more fully harmonizing our approaches to Mark's development.

The next hurdle confronting us was arranging for Mark's transportation to Lawton Elementary School, which was located 8 miles from Fort Sill. Since primary-level students residing at Fort Sill attended school on Post, there was no scheduled transportation to Lawton. I appealed to the Post commander who forthwith provided a staff car with driver to transport Mark to and from class. Lillian was greatly encouraged by this exceptional gesture of support as well as the prospect of a brighter future for Mark under the tutelage of this special teacher.

Almost concurrently, Kym qualified for early enrollment in kindergarten despite being underage. This daily respite from full-time childcare afforded Lillian a short-lived season of emotional well-being. For several weeks, all went well for Mark. His first driver seemed to be instinctively sensitive to Mark's moods and quirks. Mark's moments of defiance were appropriately ignored or judiciously pacified. There were even days when the driver apparently deciphered the core of Mark's behavior code. On these days, such a rapport was established that full-speed-ahead development seemed to be on the horizon.

The new teacher was good for Mark. She was blessed with a high threshold for frustration that simply overwhelmed those in her custody. To put it simply: They could not break her and soon the students had the reassurance of knowing that fact. She was not going to give up on them. In fact, she saw that her first task was validation of abnormal behavior. She staunchly refused to equate behavior and value. Every student's value was unassailable, no matter what they might do in class.

Mark's obstinacy was the teacher's biggest challenge. She had anticipated his physical limitations. Her observation of him at dinner had convinced her that he was capable of learning, albeit at a slower rate. She had to figure out how to adapt to his system of approaching the world and his responses to various prompts. At the same time, she had to manage his mood swings and natural childishness. Her initial strategy was to let him range unconstrained while randomly interrupting his self-initiated activity with nonthreatening, quick-reaction assignments. These tasks were progressive and designed to gradually build structure. Apparently, this methodology was not the result of any formal training. She had settled on this course of action simply because it made sense to her. However, she quickly learned that Mark's conduct did not respond to a predictable formula. She could not simply modify the flow of his behavior. He did what he chose to do. She had to deal with him as best she could.

Right away, I realized that she could communicate with Mark better than we could. Our body language, when responding to problem behavior, often conveyed our frustration. We left Mark little chance of discerning whether we were upset with the behavior or with him. This was particularly a problem with Lillian's scolding, since she bore the brunt of parenting. Of course, Lillian and I had a deep and abiding love for all of our children, but I'm sure that more than once Mark must have felt that we had found him personally unworthy. I deeply regretted that we were falling into that pattern over and over again. I was so thankful that he had this new teacher in his life, who seemed to have an instinctive gift for expressing personal support and affection for all of her students—even as she tried her best to shape their behavior.

Then, in early January 1962, I left the family again to begin the Fort Bliss phase of my Career Course.

13

Sufficient Grace

Husbands, love your wives, just as Christ loved the church.
Paul's letter to the Ephesians 5:25

I can do all things through him who strengthens me.
Philippians 4:13

My home away from home for three months was the Air Defense Center and School at Fort Bliss, the sprawling northeast neighbor of El Paso. There was no option to bring Lillian with me. During this temporary duty, all Career Course students were housed in student Bachelor Officer Quarters (BOQ).

We "Cannon Cockers" were now out of our element. For the first time in my career, I had to compete with Air Defense Artillery officers on their turf. The Career Course orientation now shifted from the Field Artillery intricacies of targeting people and installations on the ground to destroying airborne intruders. The ever-increasing speed and maneuverability of incoming aircraft and missiles introduced new challenges in modern warfare. The ground component's role was no less important, but Air Defense had to dramatically upgrade their capabilities in order to defeat platforms of destruction traveling at supersonic speeds. Comprehending these highly sophisticated command-and-control systems was a whole new ballgame for me. The Air Defense contingent, frequently the object of friendly taunts by Field Artillery-types for being "pie-in-the-sky soldiers," relished the fact that it was comeuppance time for the Cannon Cockers. The terms "Nike" and "Hawk" became the new hallmarks of artillery warfare conducted in the airspace over the battlefield. Despite the challenge of this push-button warfare, I was more convinced than ever that I had chosen wisely when I selected terra-firma-based Field Artillery for my career.

My actual training turned out to be less than captivating—but Fort Bliss would soon prove to be the setting for the pivotal event of my life.

On Monday, February 12, 1962, I visited the Air Defense Center library for the first time. Sitting alone at a table in the reference section was a classmate whom I had seen before but had never met. As I took the seat across from him, I could not help noticing that this classmate was unusually engaged. He was unabashedly reading the Bible. There was even a slight hint of a smile on his face as he continued to read without looking up. For a moment, I flashed back to the chaplain's office at West Point. I recalled those devotional sessions as times of healing and renewal. Each had been a "bridge over troubled waters." I had missed the fellowship with likeminded cadets. Now I sensed a special kinship to this stranger who had staked out his own spiritual oasis in this highly unlikely place.

I introduced myself to Bob Schneider, an Air Defense artilleryman from Minnesota. Bob was an ROTC graduate from the University of Minnesota who had spent his entire career on Air Defense assignments while I had been working in Field Artillery. We began talking about what Bob was reading. Soon, I was talking about my own affinity for the great truths of the Bible but acknowledged that, under the press of career and family demands, there had been a lapse in my spiritual life. Bob identified with me by giving a mini testimony of his life. Then, he mostly listened to my story while at the same time taking my spiritual temperature. At the conclusion of our visit, Bob surmised that I was still in the spiritually searching mode and had not made a truly life-changing leap of faith.

We met again the next day in a tactics class. We were members of a team whose assignment was to allocate Air Defense elements to the field commander conducting a mobile defense. Bob was the only career Air Defense artilleryman on our team. Being the expert, he became the de facto team leader. It quickly became evident that Bob was a brilliant tactician. But much more apparent was his affinity for people. Rather than dictate the solution to a given scenario, he preferred to be the catalyst for group attainment of the solution. I would soon learn that his unobtrusive classroom deportment was a carryover from his highly practiced style of witnessing his faith. I would also discover that Bob's allegiance to the

Army, his livelihood, was secondary to his vision of the Army as a uniquely fertile field for spreading the Gospel of Jesus Christ.

After class, Bob invited me to join him for lunch. While enjoying a mutual favorite, creamed beef on toast, Bob talked about his family: his wife, Gloria, twin daughters and a son. Just listening to Bob talk about his faith and his family left an indelible impression on me. Here was a man truly living his priorities. He lived out his Christian values like no one I had ever met. As a natural extension of our mutual esteem for the Bible, Bob invited me to attend a meeting of the Fort Bliss chapter of the Officer's Christian Union (OCU) scheduled for that same evening.

The OCU was an international organization of military officers committed to spreading the Gospel throughout the world's officer corps. It had been founded by British officers during the mid-19th century. Chapters had been established on almost every major military installation of the U.S. armed forces. Membership was not extended to the enlisted ranks based on the premise that many tradition-bound officers would consider it inimical to good order and discipline to be so intimately bonded to the rank and file. Exclusion had nothing to do with class or status. The founders had unequivocally embraced the fact that Christ was no respecter of persons but had reasoned that the best way to reach the entire profession of arms for Christ was through the leadership. In their collective wisdom, it followed that the best format for luring hardcore authority figures was to provide an environment as free of social encumbrances as possible.

As was customary, the meeting took place at the home of one of the members stationed at Fort Bliss. After a brief period of introductions, there was a short business meeting. The host then led a time of prayer and praise followed by Bible study. Consistent with the OCU norm, there were a dozen participants, including wives. After a concluding prayer, there was ample opportunity for fellowship over coffee and dessert. Four of the participants, including Bob and myself, were classmates in our program. Never before had I experienced such a power-packed sense of oneness among men who hardly knew one another.

I now looked forward to these weekly gatherings. Meeting locations were rotated amongst the permanent membership. I was also getting to know others who, like Bob, were some of God's special ambassadors. To say that Bob's faith and his career expertise made him charismatic understated his stature among us. Many other officers were struck by his aptitude for drawing people into his circle. I recognized that as a Christ-likeness he had developed over the years. Even among those who mocked his Christianity, he was not shaken.

Energized by Bob and the OCU experience, I began to review my performance critically as a husband and father. *Had I fulfilled my Bible-directed role as a spiritual leader in my family?* Clearly, the answer was no. *Had I been the kind of husband that the Apostle Paul described in the book of Ephesians?* The answer came to me as a lukewarm—sometimes. *Was I raising my children with a proper respect for the Lord? Did my brand of nurturing breed resentment and anger in the children?* At best, I could not be sure. I had considered these and other similar questions before, but for the first time I knew where to find answers.

While contemplating these matters in the solitude of my room, I was suddenly caught up in the realization that my life had changed forever. At that very moment, I invited Christ to take charge of my life!

A constant foursome sprang from these connections in OCU and our coursework: Bob, Carl Smith, Ed Rushkowski and me. We studied together, ate together and grew together spiritually. Despite racial, cultural and temperamental differences, we were absolutely one in the eternal scheme of things. We hungered for and shared in the Bread of Life. We were even able to set aside our differences in our denominational backgrounds. We trusted in, clung to and relied on the Bible as the sole authority for doctrine and reproof. It was my earnest desire that my decision for Christ would reign over all the icons of the world. I now knew that, apart from Christ, I could do nothing—but with Christ, all things were possible.

I was longing to share this new awareness—this spiritual rebirth—with Lillian. Over and over again, I thought about how to express the fullness of my encounter with Christ with pen and paper. Ultimately, I concluded that such a letter would only confuse her and raise anxious questions. I knew that she would want to look into my eyes as we talked about this face to face. Where had this rebirth originated? Would her role in my life somehow be different now? I even wondered whether she would connect my Christian awakening with Mark's condition. Was I chasing miracles now? I decided it would be best to wait for my return to Fort Sill to give a full accounting of this new covenant with Christ. She could see my earnestness if we were facing each other and she could search my face for confirmation. I planned the conversation to the smallest detail—even my reassuring caress of her hand as I would tell her that I loved her more than ever.

The final weeks of our course were a flurry of activity. All of my classmates were anxiously anticipating their next assignments. In my case, I had been prompted by my Artillery branch personnel officer to apply for civil schooling. If accepted, I would be one of a select few to be sent by the Army to earn a master's degree at a designated university. Three weeks before graduation, I received orders assigning me to the Student Detachment, Headquarters Sixth Army, stationed at the University of Arizona in Tucson. I had hoped to pursue a master's in political science, but my orders came through with an assignment to earn a master's in mechanical engineering. I was surprised but delighted. I was one of six U.S. Army officers given these two-year assignments to the University of Arizona.

So, when I finally returned to Lillian and the children on April 19, 1962, our reunion was charged with suspense and emotion. So much had happened to me! So much had happened to Lillian and the children! There were stories to share and plans to be made for the next move. First and foremost was sharing news about the children. The stories Lillian told me made it clear that Kym was as spunky as ever. Jennifer was as bright and cuddly as any 1-year-old could be. There had been slight improvement in Mark's social skills, but the prognosis for development was less than encouraging.

Lillian was noticeably thinner. My concerns about what seemed to be her frailty were repeatedly deflected by Lillian. She insisted that she was as healthy and happy as ever. Good order reigned in our household. Finally, I found a moment to begin telling her about the experiences that had spiritually transformed me at Fort Bliss. I reached out and took both of her hands. Just as I had planned, I tried to speak with intensity and certitude.

My eyes looked into her eyes. When I finished, there was silence.

Lillian slowly withdrew her hands as she kept gazing into my eyes. Still, she said nothing. It was not that she questioned my sincerity, but she realized that I had passed through a narrow gate and she wondered if she could come along. She knew about my Christian fellowship at West Point and, as a family, we had always supported the chapel wherever we were based. But, this was different. My voice had a new ring of commitment. Perhaps by divine intervention, I knew what she was thinking: Would she now have to play second fiddle to my newly found spirituality? Was this yet another weight on her shoulders?

I realized that I would have to place a higher priority on nurturing our relationship. I would need to, in effect, love away her apprehensions.

There were countless opportunities to do that on our immediate horizon. We had to pack up the household, once again. Then, we endured two hard days of travel from Fort Sill to the Davis-Monthan Air Force Base, which would be our temporary home as we looked for more permanent quarters in Tucson. I was thankful, and surprised, that the children posed no problem at all. The monotony of the scrubby desert seemed to have a calming effect even on the highly charged Kym. As we negotiated mile after mile of patchy brush, we all shared our disappointment at the landscape. We had envisioned dramatic desert vistas we had seen in Hollywood movies. This seemed to be a wasteland.

Davis-Monthan Air Force Base was located just east of the city of Tucson. It was an Air Force logistics center and home for mothballed tactical and strategic aircraft. Acres of fighters, bombers, and support airplanes were parked in orderly array, awaiting their destiny. As we rolled into the base, I kept praying that God would lead us to suitable housing. In fact, I was strengthened by my awareness that the Schneiders and other members of OCU were praying along with us across every mile. So, it seemed providential that a West Point classmate, Bob Blum, was finishing up a similar course of study at the university and agreed to help us look for housing.

When we arrived at temporary quarters, Bob insisted upon picking up the family for dinner at his home. Expressing her misgivings privately to me, Lillian scrambled to get herself and the children ready for a meal at the home of people who were perfect strangers—just an hour after arriving at the base.

Bob's warmth and casual manner did much to relieve Lillian's discomfort. Bob and Ann Blum had three children: Jennifer, Mark and John. Over and above the commonality of names, the birth years of the Blum and Worthy youngsters were nearly identical. After introductions, Lillian and Ann were caught up in the frenzy of last-minute preparations for the big meal. Bob and I reminisced a bit but quickly became absorbed in what I could expect at the university. The focal point for the children was the Blum's German Shepherd, named Coffee. Mark was guarded at first, but soon sensed that Coffee was no threat. As soon as Mark realized that these new children were not placing any demands on him, he exuberantly joined in their activities.

At times, Lillian seemed almost mesmerized by the ambience of the Blum home. It was evident that she and Ann shared a penchant for order and good taste. Nothing was overstated. There was an uncontrived casual elegance that reflected the character of the householders. Despite the emphasis on the informal in their interactions with us, exquisite touches were displayed throughout the home. Lillian marveled at the similarity of tastes she shared with Ann. At the same time, both of us were struck by the contrasts in our families. It was obvious to us that the Blums loved each other and were a close-knit family, but they were much more relaxed around each other than Lillian and I were when visitors came to our home. This was partly due to Mark's amazing ease in playing with these new friends. He loved the evening so much that he cried when it was time to leave.

Before we parted, Bob arranged for me to meet another Army student, Howard Jelinek, to help with finding a rental near the university. Howard was West Point Class of '52. Like Bob, he was finishing up his degree requirements. He had managed to rent a place just a couple of blocks from campus. His landlady, a long-retired school teacher, also owned a three-bedroom ranch next door. When I saw the place, I was pleased. The rent was reasonable and the walking distance to school was value added. Finally, I faced the owner, who proved to be a withered little nonagenarian who put me through a grilling the likes of which I had rarely endured. I felt she was peering into my innermost being as her eyes searched my face the whole time we talked. When she ran out of questions, she coolly offered me cookies. I guessed that meant I had met with her approval. After this moment of hospitality, she served up a handwritten rental agreement, which I signed. I walked away with enormous respect for her.

The university's ROTC building—the oldest on campus—was the administrative hub for all military students. There, I met the ROTC commander and senior faculty member for military affairs. After the usual introductions and courtesies, I was turned over to an assistant who advised me on registration and took me on an abbreviated tour of the university. Afterward, I returned to Howard's home, where I met his wife and three of their five children. Throughout the visit, his wife never left her seat on the sofa. Her pet bulldog never left her side. She never spoke except when spoken to and stared at me the whole time, as if I were a creature from a different planet. Howard ignored her behavior and busied himself trying to sell me textbooks and other materials that he would no longer need. All of his assistance amounted to a savvy business proposition for Howard. I had learned that the landlady was paying him a signing bonus for having brought her a new tenant. Try as I might, I could not feel an ounce of gratitude for Howard's efforts. I was convinced that apart from the monetary benefits that accrued to him as a result of our association, Howard saw me as a nonentity.

Whatever forces had led us to this new home on North Martin Street, Lillian was pleased. She was particularly thankful that she could have the car every day. My ability to walk home for lunch was another unexpected bonus. The two large palm trees in the front yard and the orange trees all around the neighborhood fascinated her. Thanks to the extremely low humidity, air-conditioning was not required. A roof-mounted water cooler kept the inside of the house comfortable. There was a small backyard and covered arbor where the children could play without supervision. The Davis-Monthan Base Exchange and hospital were just 20 minutes away and would provide for most of her household needs. The local supermarket was just two blocks north. She would have to shop around for a beauty salon. Except for our isolation from other military families, she was completely satisfied with her new surroundings.

Lillian focused on getting the children registered in the new school system as I settled into the university along with the other military students. Much to my surprise and delight, I spotted another familiar face: Capt. Jim Dozier, former personnel officer of the 2nd Squadron, 2nd Armored Cavalry Regiment. We had left Bamberg within two weeks of each other. Jim had just graduated from the Armor career course at Fort Knox. After exchanging greetings and family updates, Jim introduced me to his friend, Capt. George Loffert, West Point Class of '56. Our meeting was indeed a fateful moment. Although we could tell that the chemistry was right for friendship—none of us realized that we would spend the majority of our waking hours together over the next two years.

The three of us went through the formal registration process together, being careful to sign up for the same classes. At the time, I was unaware of the fact that both George and Jim had graduated from West Point with academic standings considerably higher than mine. All three of us had been advised to sign up immediately for a calculus refresher course during that first summer session. At the last minute, a second calculus class was established because of unexpected student demand. In the process, I was separated from Jim and George. My initial disappointment turned to thankfulness when the student grapevine began passing stories about Jim and George's instructor, a Chinese professor named Louise C. Lim. Dr. Lim was a brilliant mathematician who had little tolerance for those less intellectually blessed. She taught as if her class was the only one needed to meet degree requirements. Jim and George would suffer but survive. I too would struggle in calculus, even under a less demanding instructor. I doubt that I could have survived the scrutiny of the redoubtable Dr. Lim.

The fall semester brought together all of the remaining military students. There was comfort in numbers, especially in light of the variety of backgrounds and levels of academic acumen of my peers. Most had completed their undergraduate work several years earlier. All armed services were represented. All were engineering students. A lot of our conversations in those first few weeks involved mourning our disadvantage as returning students, compared with younger students fresh from their undergraduate classes. A lot of the anxiety centered on professors like Dr. Lim, who were notoriously rigorous and refused to cut the older students any slack. They seemed to us to take pleasure in publicly demonstrating our limitations. We all were encouraged when we learned that there were several ex-military instructors in the engineering department. Surely, their presence would make a difference, we reasoned.

Truth be told, the military students included some remarkable scholars. During Bob Blum's two years in the advanced schooling program, he had survived Dr. Lim—and had successfully completed the requirements for master's degrees in both operations research and nuclear engineering. He would subsequently receive his doctorate and after retiring from the Army, go on to seminary and become an Episcopal priest.

Jim, George and I became a threesome. So did our spouses: Lillian, Judy Dozier and Gloria Loffert. They had much in common. Each had small children. Each had a love for West Point. All were career Army wives. Gloria's Hispanic heritage added a welcome cross-cultural dimension to their friendship. The only downside to our relationships was the distance between our residences. Because I was within walking distance of campus, Lillian always had a car and often was called upon to chauffeur her friends. As a threesome, they made sure that Tucson had few secrets. Gloria was even able to breach some of the inner circles of the city's considerable Hispanic community.

Ann Blum advised us to enroll Kym in the parochial school run by Saint Michael and All Angels Episcopal Church—then she went to considerable lengths to make it happen. There was a daunting waiting list to get into the school, but Ann already had clawed out an opening for her Jennifer. The Blums were moving away but she extracted a promise from Lillian that she would pursue a slot for Kym by whatever means necessary. Even after she left, Ann went as far as to intercede for Kym's acceptance in a letter to the vicar and headmaster, Father Francis Fowler. As it turned out, Kym's acceptance was assured once Father Fowler learned that we were a black family. A social liberal but a staunch behaviorist conservative, Father Fowler welcomed the opportunity to integrate his school as long as the parents shared his traditional views on child-nurturing. A blustery and sometimes irreverent taskmaster, Father Fowler ran his church and school with an iron hand. He walked with an exaggerated limp of unknown origin, almost always carrying a swagger stick and accompanied by an oversized French poodle named Sam. When he entered a classroom, the children would jump to their feet and not make a sound unless spoken to. His well-used swagger stick was a constant reminder of his unswerving insistence upon good manners and obedience. He was a strong advocate of daily homework as appropriate confirmation that learning was, indeed, taking place.

Saint Michael and All Angels was in large part an edifice whose physical and spiritual character was a direct reflection of Father Fowler. Its

Spanish-style adobe construction was reminiscent of Catholic missions in the Southwest. This was what would be called today an Anglo-Catholic parish with Episcopal liturgies close to their Roman Catholic origins. Ritualistic discipline permeated every aspect of the Church and school. It was Father Fowler's way or no way. This was the environment surrounding Kym's introduction to the world of learning. Kym loved it. Lillian was delighted.

Mark was another matter. Other than an excellent Sunday school program, Saint Michael could offer nothing suitable for him. For the next two years, Lillian would have to settle for the meager special education offerings of the Tucson public school system. Appropriate and affordable private help was nonexistent. Lillian would have to carve out her own home-based program for Mark's intellectual development. The associated stress would take a terrible emotional and, ultimately, physical toll.

Jim, George, I and the other military students soon became consumed with the demands of the master's program. We studied together, ate together and together we rued the day we had voluntarily applied for civil schooling. Twelve-hour days were not uncommon. It was indeed helpful to have three ex-military officers as instructors on the staff of the engineering department. They were all sympathetic to the plight of these "elder scholars," particularly in light of the disparity in our ages and currency when compared to the other master's candidates in their classes. Most of all, they admired the work ethic of the military students.

I survived the fall semester but just barely. Jim and George fared slightly better. Though the three of us were not pleased with our performance, we were relieved that it was over. We had been through the fire and while we had not emerged unscathed, like heat-treated steel, we were better prepared for the tests ahead. The next several months would be critical as we took the initial steps toward completing our theses. We would have to explore possible subjects, ascertain, then gain commitments to use appropriate facilities on campus—and lock in a thesis advisor. All of the above had to be accomplished concurrent with an upgrading of our academic performances.

While attending a series of lectures on combustion and flame theory conducted by Dr. Russell Petersen, associate professor of Aerospace and Mechanical Engineering, I decided to explore the area of flame propagation as a possible research project. After all, I was an artilleryman and controlled flame propagation was an integral part of propellant-projectile physics. Dr. Petersen had spent considerable time arguing that flame studies—to include flame speed, the limits of flame propagation and temperature profiles—are best carried out by observations of a planar flame front propagating in one dimension. A thin disc-like flame that takes up a position of equilibrium a short distance above the burner port would enable direct photographic measurement of flame velocity. Dr. Petersen had long wanted an apparatus for producing such a flame as a part of his combustion laboratory. After intense consultations and corroboration of my potential for devising and fabricating the necessary hardware, I was given the go-ahead to design and construct a flat flame burner to fulfill my thesis requirement. Dr. Petersen consented to be my advisor.

Dr. Petersen seemed to perfectly fit the stereotype of the brilliant academician who is a bumbling misfit outside the environs of the classroom. Even his professional colleagues regarded him as a social pariah. He was not unaware of their snubs and, in fact, seemed to relish their discomfort when they were forced to deal with him. The military students seemed to gravitate toward him and vice versa. George speculated that this was due to one misfit's natural affinity for another.

I discovered that Dr. Petersen loved to play handball. Soon, we established a regular foursome. Round-robin play dictated that each would have the dubious honor of playing with the professor from time to time. He was a lousy player but admired by all for his enthusiasm. A thoroughly enjoyable eccentric, his military students began to include him in other social events. To reciprocate, he invited me, Jim, George and a few others to his home for dinner. It was truly an evening to remember.

Lillian and I were the first to arrive. I rightly surmised that this would not be a night of eloquence and gentility when we heard at least two dogs barking and children squealing as we approached the house. Standing at the front door, we heard a loud, "Shut up and open the door!"

A frail and tousled youngster opened the door and just stared as we entered the foyer. Two mutts slid menacingly across the floor toward us. A large tomcat was perched on a high-backed chair at the entrance to the living room. A caged bird yelled, "Hi there!"

Lillian was stupefied as she surveyed the total disarray that surrounded us while trying to dodge kids swooping down on us from every direction. And still there was no sign of our hosts. After I had counted five more children in addition to the one who opened the door, an equally unkempt Mrs. Petersen breezed into the room. While making no apologies for herself, the children, animals or the general disorder, she could not have been more gracious. Lillian's consternation immediately began to wither away, except for a persisting regret that she had wasted so much time and effort to be appropriately attired.

One half hour after all the other guests had arrived, Dr. Petersen strolled in. An apology for being late was mouthed but projected no great relevance. After introductions all around, the children were shunted off to an unknown destination and dinner was served. Despite mismatched Melmac dishes and flatware, the dinner was simple but outstanding. The Petersens were a totally compatible and fun-filled pair entirely without guile or pretense. While Mrs. Petersen was clearing the dishes, Russ departed to the back porch from which he retrieved a huge watermelon for dessert. There was stunned silence as his guests watched him prop the melon on his knee and proceed to make the initial cut. Before the knife had sunk more than an inch into the melon, Jim leaped to his rescue with an urgent but diplomatic offer to finish the job. His initiative was based upon his contention that all Floridians were uniquely skilled in the art of "watermelon segmenting." All in all, it was an evening that no one would ever forget.

Tucson was not all work and no play. There were many interesting places to visit that could be enjoyed in one day. Whenever my studies would permit, the family would schedule a trip to one of the local points of interest. The Saguaro National Monument was the first on our list. Acres of giant saguaro cactus dotted the landscape, projecting an eerie kind of beauty, much like tombstones crisscrossing a graveyard. Their prickly fluted stems curled upwards like candelabras, sometimes reaching 40 or 50 feet in the air. One could not help being awed by the hardiness of these spectacular specimens. After the visit, Lillian could no longer scornfully refer to "the abominable desert." She had now come face to face with its grandeur.

Mount Lemmon was equally fascinating. Situated about a half-hour's drive to the north from the city limits of Tucson, Mt. Lemmon was an anomalous oasis of lush foliage rising up out of arid and patchy earth. Tall pines and the dense carpeting of other vegetation were a breathtaking contrast to the desert. A ski run accentuated the meteorological contrasts between the Tucsonian valley and the rim of mountains, of which Mount Lemmon was the most accessible. It was not unusual for the temperature to be 30 degrees cooler on Mount Lemmon. Tucsonians boasted that they could escape from objectionable heat any time they desired.

Nogales, a border town in the Mexican state of Sonora, was situated about 60 miles to the south. Albeit on a lesser scale, Nogales was a shopper's delight, especially for those who, like me, enjoyed haggling. Working as a team, Lillian would identify what she wanted, and I would consummate the deal. Many "treasures" found their way back to Tucson where Lillian, Judy and Gloria would subsequently compare notes and exchange tips on where to find the best buys. It took three trips to Nogales before we realized that we were more often than not the victims rather than the victors in our bartering with the street merchants.

There were also visits to Fort Huachuca, Arizona, the home of the United States Army Electronics Command located about 70 miles to the south and east of Tucson. Aside from providing an alternative to the offerings of the Post Exchange and commissary at Davis-Monthan, Fort Huachuca was located in the heart of one of the best recreational areas in the state of Arizona. Hunting and fishing were excellent. The moderate climate was conducive to camping and other outdoor activities. Because of its affordability, Fort Huachuca became a popular weekend haven for military families. The Worthys, Doziers and Lofferts were no exceptions. Adding to its unique allure for us was the fact that Fort Huachuca had been the home of the all-black 92nd Division during World War II. Much to my disappointment, we could find no vestiges commemorating its earlier association with the 92nd.

As the school year wore on, Lillian's preoccupation with Mark was no less intense than my commitment to achieving my academic objectives. Neither she nor I appreciated the debilitating effect of the stress from her daily encounters with Mark's obstinacy. Jennifer continued to be a delightfully happy child and Kym's waywardness was more often than not swallowed up by her many hours under the regimen of St. Michael's. The near idyllic circumstances surrounding the rearing of Kym and Jennifer further served to exaggerate the Lillian's feeling of frustration in her coping with Mark.

Lillian's physical stress finally reached a crisis point on an otherwise enjoyable Saturday evening. We had decided to enjoy a movie at the base theater and we were returning home when, without warning, Lillian began to writhe in pain. So severe were her stomach cramps that I immediately whirled the car around and headed for the Davis-Monthan Hospital emergency room. Lillian was quickly admitted and began to undergo a series of tests and evaluations that would last for two weeks. When all the test results were in, the verdict was that her long-running struggles with a duodenal ulcer had resurfaced. I was startled to read the lengthy medical report, which reminded me that her symptoms had been going on, to a greater or lesser degree, for six years. Now, she was down to 95 pounds and the doctors were recommending surgery.

I was worried. We prayed. Our whole focus became resolving this painful problem that Lillian had been wrestling with on a daily basis for years. Six weeks later, she was readmitted to the hospital for corrective surgery. Doctors removed two-thirds of her ulcerated stomach. The surgery went well and I was hugely relieved to see her wake up in the recovery area. She gave me a reassuring smile but said nothing. After a prayer of thanksgiving, I went to share the news with concerned friends who had shown up in the hospital waiting room to support us.

One week later, Lillian was released to go home. For two days, I had spent every available moment cleaning the house and washing clothes in an attempt to maintain her standards for housekeeping. I wanted to discourage any anxiety she might have that she needed to become prematurely active around the house. Gloria and Judy had been immensely helpful to me and insisted on taking turns staying with her during the day, despite her objections. The friend "on duty" would bring food for us while the other would entertain all the children at their house. This arrangement lasted six days. Finally, Lillian thanked them profusely while pretending to order them out of her house.

Recovery was swift. Lillian had never felt better. The children had never been better behaved. My workload was manageable despite the added burdens. Everything seemed to fall into place. Lillian had resolved not to drift back into her old pattern of stress and anxiety. She told me that she was resolved to approach her caring for Mark one day at a time. She would do what she could to meet his needs but not at the expense of her own well-being or that of the rest of the family.

I quickly noticed the difference. Instead of the familiar roller coaster of emotional response to Mark's flare-ups, Lillian now seemed to respond with a confident aura of appropriate concern mingled with a new detachment. Now, after one of Mark's eruptions, which once had touched off fireworks in our home, Lillian would tell me, "He'll get over it."

I flashed back to that doctor whose advice we had dismissed years ago. He had advised us,

"Let him do what he wants to do. Don't try to restrain him. Let him act it out."

At the time, I thought the doctor was a quack. I wasn't ready to hear such advice. Now, I thought that doctor was prophetic, because Mark seemed no worse for Lillian's new laid-back responses toward his tantrums. Gradually, Mark showed us that he noticed the difference as well. He seemed baffled by her new lack of full-scale engagement when he erupted. There was no way for him to win this contest of wills, because Mom was refusing to play. That is probably why Mark began to focus his aggravation on me. I followed Lillian's example and Mark soon learned that he could not prompt an emotional outburst from either father or mother.

I had a nagging suspicion that this was too good to be true—and it was. Our carefully modulated responses all went up in smoke one day when Mark's emotional outburst reached the point that he crashed through the screen door. Initially stunned and frightened by what he had just done, he began running down the street. Lillian lost her composure. She frantically chased him, caught him and brought him home in an emotional struggle. Mark realized he had pushed a new button. A few days later, he repeated this explosive new provocation. A third episode occurred when I was at home and, like Lillian, I lost all reserve in response. Our old doubts and fears resurfaced. The walls of carefully practiced tranquility came tumbling down.

That was an anxious autumn. On Friday, November 22, 1963, I was having lunch with Jim when an eerie hush settled over the cafeteria. The news spread table to table: President John F. Kennedy had been shot. No one knew what to say. Even Walter Cronkite searched for words to describe the moment. Instinctively, the military students on campus descended on the ROTC building. That's where we ultimately heard the news that the president had died. A military student ball had been scheduled for that same evening. When one of the students naively broke the somber spell by asking about the final arrangements for the evening gala, he was soundly admonished by the colonel for not realizing the obvious. The ball would be cancelled. The commander-in-chief was dead.

As the weeks passed, my thesis project was winding down. After designing and constructing the flat flame burner, I had reached the point of drawing conclusions and making recommendations for further study. I had begun my work with a historical sketch of previous investigations of the flat flame burner with emphasis upon the more imaginative innovations and the synthesis of these ideas in succeeding studies. The general theory was interwoven into this historical sketch, including a short treatise on the aerodynamics of flame propagation. This was followed by specifics on design and assembly of the system supplemented by appropriate figures and tables.

The design and construction of the burner were rudimentary. The results, however, showed that the concept was sound enough to warrant more sophisticated extensions of the system. My burner had represented the foundation for combustion studies encompassing a substantial portion of the less-investigated areas of laminated flame propagation.

Dr. Petersen was clearly pleased with the results. While my design had not achieved all of Dr. Petersen's objectives, it had made a significant contribution to his dream of a combustion laboratory equal to that found in any university in the country.

The defense of my thesis was the next hurdle. This involved an appearance before a thesis review committee that was convened to confirm my grasp of the research. The committee drew professors whose disciplines were related to the subject. The success of my defense rested in no small part on the academic egos of my interrogators. All of the advanced degree candidates shuddered in fear that we would have to stand before the likes of Dr. Lim. Sadistic wagers were made among aspirants as to who would have to suffer the slings and arrows of the infamous mathematician.

One day, written notifications of committee assignments were posted. Jim and George were standing at the department bulletin board as I approached. The look on their faces signaled disaster. As I read for myself, my worst fears were confirmed. I, alone among all candidates, had been assigned Dr. Lim as part of my thesis review committee. The fact that I was the only one of my associates who had not previously suffered under Dr. Lim only served to intensify my horror. Neither Jim nor George made any attempt to soften the blow. Words of consolation eluded them; joking would have been cruelly inappropriate.

"I guess lunch is on me," I finally murmured, shaking my head wearily at my fate.

As I walked in the door later that evening, Lillian knew that calamity had struck in a big way. She had seen that look on my face only once before. It had been that fearful night of November 11, 1953, when I emerged from that restaurant in Clayton, New Mexico. Now, as then, she said nothing.

As I shared the frightful prospects of my pending encounter with the venerable Dr. Lim, Lillian could not completely suppress a derisive smile. "Surely, you're overstating the case," she said. "How could one little old professor strike such fear in you?" She began to coach me. Dr. Lim could not singlehandedly invalidate my exhaustive efforts. She reminded me that I was the author of this thesis. I was the one who built this apparatus and no one, not even Dr. Petersen, knew as much about it as I did.

Thus reassured, I began to feel some relief. But, before retiring for the evening, I prayed fervently:

> *Lord Jesus, I thank You that I am privileged to be able to come to You as my Father. I thank You for Your love, Your faithfulness, Your mercy, Your grace and Your forgiveness. I thank You for my family. I thank You for providing for my every need. Forgive me for needing to be reminded of Your omnipresence, Your omnipotence and Your omniscience. Lord Jesus, I again come to You seeking Holy Spirit direction. I know that You understand my concerns better than me. Your Word admonishes us to pray about everything, worry about nothing, tell You our needs, and then to thank You for Your answers. Though unmerited, You have*

*graciously made provision for meeting our needs when You tell us,
'Ask and you shall receive that your joy may be full.' Right now, I
claim that promise. Likewise, I am comforted when I recall Your
proclamation, 'If I am for you, who can be against you?' And I
know that I am divinely empowered when I appropriate the
miracle: 'I can do all things through Christ who strengthens me.'
Lord Jesus, if it be Your will, equip me to justify the work You
have sent me here to do. Stand with me as I stand before those
who will test me. May the victory and glory be Yours. In Your
name, it is settled. Amen!*

When I walked into the classroom reserved for my defense, I saw that
chairs and tables were arranged in a semi-circle facing a wall of blackboards. Dr. Petersen, as chairman, was seated at the center table. As I
stood in front of this group, Dr. Petersen opened the proceedings by intro-
ducing me to each of the five other members of the committee. Dr. Lim
sat on the right of Dr. Petersen.

"Our purpose today is to have Capt. Worthy share with us his vision
and analysis relating to the design and construction of a flat flame burner.
It was at my suggestion that Capt. Worthy undertake this project, which
I have carefully monitored since its inception. It is my opinion that he has
more than met our jointly established objectives."

That was promising. Then, Dr. Petersen said, "Our review is scheduled to last two hours. We will begin with a 30-minute project summary
by Capt. Worthy followed by any questions and comments you deem
appropriate."

He motioned in my direction. "Captain, tell us about your burner."

Just as Dr. Petersen had coached me, I began by quoting the abstract
and introduction to my thesis, careful to maintain eye contact with the
professors. This was followed by an accounting of the general considerations and theory, burner system design and assembly, and operation
of the burner and test results. One hour had passed before I had made
any comments concerning conclusions and recommendations for further
study. I made liberal use of the blackboard for graphic impact. The length
of my remarks was a clear violation of the previously stated ground rules,

but this strategy was no accident. I was following the script devised earlier by Dr. Petersen.

Finally, Dr. Petersen interrupted me to declare that the remaining time would be devoted to questions. As chairman, he began the questioning. My answer led to a subsequent question by Dr. Petersen. The second question was crafted to lead to a third question that only Dr. Petersen could logically ask. And so it went. Dr. Petersen's questioning was so skillfully managed that even I was unaware that no one else, including Dr. Lim, could justify intrusion into the analytical domain so carefully developed by the chairman.

After 2 hours, 15 minutes, Dr. Petersen apologized for running over-time and announced that if there were no further questions, I should leave the room while they considered the veracity of my representation of my project.

Neither Dr. Lim, nor anyone else, had asked a single question! Despite my relief over not having to take on Dr. Lim, I still wondered about my performance. Just as I began to pray—thanking God for bringing me through the fire—Dr. Petersen emerged from the conference room and beckoned me to return. Dr. Petersen was fearfully solemn as he led me to the center of the room. It was only after I had assumed my previous posture of inquisition that Dr. Petersen smiled and extended his hand amidst congratulations from the other members of the committee, including Dr. Lim.

It was over! I whispered an inaudible, *"Thank you, Jesus!"*

I debated whether to telephone Lillian or wait to tell her until I got home and decided this would be all the sweeter if I could tell her in person. Lillian had been so confident that all would go well that, as soon as I left for my defense, she began preparing a special meal to celebrate. She pulled out all the stops! She brought out the china, crystal, silver, linen and candles. Timing was the only problem. She couldn't know with certainty when I would return.

She had just stepped back from the table to critique her arrangements and check her appearance when I walked through the door. I had planned to feign a hangdog look of disappointment, but my excitement was so great that I failed miserably to tease her in that way. We burst into laughter simultaneously as I lifted her off the floor and executed a Lillian-style pirouette with her clasped in my arms.

Dinner and conversation consumed the next two hours without serious interruption from the children. Upon reflection, it was clear to me that Dr. Petersen had decided that in no way would he risk invalidation of my project by inappropriate challenge in any form. Both Lillian and I were convinced that Dr. Petersen sincerely believed that his oversight of the project had been of such depth that no one was qualified to rule unfavorably. We had always admired his brilliance. Now we would be eternally grateful for his wisdom. The rest of the evening was spent in an attitude of praise and thanksgiving.

As our evening ended, I knelt in prayer:

> *We praise You, Lord. We bless You, Lord, for You are a great God. You are a merciful God. You are a loving Father. Thank You for Your faithfulness. What a comfort it is to know that You are still in charge—that You are sovereign over all. Your grace is sufficient. We want to please You above all else. Hear our prayer. Watch over our children. We need You every hour. Bless Your holy name. Now Father, grant us the wisdom, patience, love and understanding that would make us Christ-centered parents. We yield totally to Your will for our lives. All of this we ask in the precious name of Jesus, Amen!*

Cliff, Lillian, Mark and Jennifer.

14

Successful Integration

I think every child has a life force struggling toward self-realization despite any handicap of body or mind—and given the right surroundings, will grow. ... I believe that sympathy, sincerity and service can be made to bear fruit in the lives of the children.

Educational pioneer Helena Devereux

I'm still convinced that we're going to achieve freedom right here in America. And I believe this because however much America has strayed away from the Declaration of Independence and the Constitution, the goal of America is freedom.

Dr. Martin Luther King Jr. in a 1967 speech in Cleveland, Ohio

The ache for home lives in all of us.

Maya Angelou

Following the awarding of our master's degrees, the contingent of officers leaving the university campus along with me were cast to the four corners of the earth. I was surprised and delighted to receive orders assigning me to the Air Defense Board at Fort Bliss.

I made the first trip to Fort Bliss alone to secure our Post housing before moving the whole family. Having been selected for promotion to major, I was given an upgrade in our quarters that thrilled Lillian as she anticipated what we could expect. So, my solo foray to Fort Bliss was to ensure that reality would meet our hopes. We had been planning to stay at the Post Guest House until our boxes and belongings arrived—then move into our housing when everything was ideally arranged. Unfortunately, there was an administrative error. There were no Guest House vacancies. Hearing that news, I was relieved that I had come alone.

After getting past the initial frustrations and apologies, I decided to go directly to our assigned quarters. Even though the place was empty, I could camp on the floor. Resigned to this frustrating turn of events, I unlocked the door and began turning on the lights. Almost immediately, someone was at the door! A neighbor had come to welcome us. Soon there were others. Before the evening ended, our new friends had provided cots, blankets, pillows, food and other essentials needed to tide us over until our own things arrived. The whole experience was a perfect affirmation of the time-tested adage that the military takes care of its own. This was quite a contrast with our reception among the civilians living near us in Tucson. Not one person from that neighborhood had gratuitously called on us during our entire two years as residents there.

That first couple to greet me on that night at Fort Bliss was the Post chaplain, Maj. John Siege, and his wife, Kate. He was a Lutheran minister from Chicago. The ages of their three children roughly mirrored those of ours. Soon, it was clear to us that God had again blessed us with special friends. Within weeks, the Sieges and the Worthys became inseparable.

There was a lot to be thankful for in this posting at Fort Bliss. Lillian and the children liked the place. I was glad to be spiritually surrounded by the Officers Christian Union, once again. Most importantly, these orders were my first assignment in which I could make use of my advanced studies. The Air Defense Board was a crucial component of the U.S. Army Test and Evaluation Command (TECOM). My initial duty was that of a test officer in the Electronic Systems Test Division (ESTD). In the course of time, I would become the chief of the ESTD.

My first assignment involved the testing of a new system to safeguard our nation by improving the coordination and control of our Air Defense missiles. This proposed new system would be called Missile Mentor (ANTSQ-51). Tests were conducted at a site in Arlington Heights, Illinois. This was a coordinated nationwide effort involving participants from the U.S. Army Missile Command, U.S. Air Force, the 45th Artillery Brigade, Hughes Aircraft Company, as well as members from TECOM and the Air Defense Board. The test team was brilliantly led by Chief Warrant

Officer John Nowicki. The results of the test affirmed the suitability of the ANTSQ-51 as a replacement for the older Missile Master.

Meanwhile, Lillian and I once again focused on caring for the children's needs, which meant our highest priority was finding the best resources for Mark. Kym and Jennifer both were blossoming and seemed none the worse for our lopsided parental focus on Mark's needs. Once again, we had found good friends who reached out to help us. Kate Siege told us she had heard about an experimental program for special children based at a church in the area. We asked medical and social-work professionals at the Post, but none of them knew anything about it. So, tracking down someone from that program became the next challenge.

Kate's dogged persistence paid off. With her help, we found the Brown Presbyterian Church and its new program that proved to be far ahead of its time. A year earlier, the congregation had launched an innovative initiative to work with developmentally disabled children and their families. A wellness team made up of a psychiatrist, psychologist, social worker and a pediatrician engaged all family members in a collaborative form of therapy. The children attended daily classes appropriate for their needs. The professional team met bimonthly with family members both individually and collectively to discuss whatever issues were emerging.

As we expected with such a promising program, there was a waiting list. Once again, Kate stepped in with some very effective lobbying to ensure Mark was admitted. She convinced the professional team that it would reflect positively on their program to include a civilian-military component and to demonstrate racial inclusion. Even Kym and Jennifer were invited to be part of the family interaction with the team.

This turned out to be more challenging that we expected. Baring the family soul in group sessions was a painful intrusion that Lillian resisted. Lillian was not pleased that the professionals working with Mark wanted input from our other two children. Lillian thought this was too invasive of our private lives. I tried to reassure her, but she was hesitant. On their end, the clinicians did not help matters. Their facility was not designed for comfortable family interaction and the professionals' stares and awkward silences, as we talked, produced more anxiety. Lillian and I sat through some long, uncomfortable sessions before we finally made headway in opening up.

Through this agonizing process, *we* were becoming better socialized—but not Mark! Despite the noblest efforts of the team, Mark seemed to sense that he was a resident guinea pig under the critical eye of everyone around him. In my mind, I could hear him saying to all of us: "You can prod and probe my family all you want, but I won't stand for it!"

After weeks of observation and collective appraisal, it was painfully clear to everyone that the Brown experiment had met its match. From Mark, we were seeing more than mere refusal to participate. On several occasions, Mark burst out in violent episodes. In one instance, he ran down the aisles of the commissary throwing objects helter-skelter. As Lillian tried to restrain him, he hit her. Finally, Mark was subdued by several adults and was sent by ambulance to a hospital emergency room. From there, he was sent to a psychiatric ward.

The medical reports began to pile up once again. One from January 23, 1967, described "chronic brain syndrome with psychosis secondary to birth trauma; manifested by mental retardation, severe emotional liability with regressive behavior, outbursts of uncontrollable rage, delusional thinking. ... The patient needs residential treatment and will be confined here until such arrangements can be made."

Three days later, the report was that it "appears that patient will be a management problem." In particular, Mark's disruptive interactions with other patients were troubling to the staff. By January 27, his medication was strengthened. He was moved to a "seclusion room."

The reports show that the medical team kept trying to move him toward peaceful interactions with others. But, on January 31, he began throwing objects again and threatening the personnel. Most heartbreaking for Lillian and me were reports that he occasionally withdrew, crying and begging for us. Then, at other times, his behavior was explosively out of control. On February 6, this entry was made in his medical log: "Says that he can destroy everybody with his hands, claiming to be a judo expert." Obviously, Mark was not trained in martial arts and, of course, the staff knew that. But his seesawing between emotional withdrawal and violent expressions was troubling. On February 8, for example, we were riding high. The staff noted that he was very happy to see me during a visit. The next day, we crashed. He was back to throwing objects at the staff.

The emotional tug on our hearts was almost unbearable. A February 26 entry read: "Cries frequently to go home." As emotionally wrenching as this process was for all of us, we also had to admit that Mark's erratic behavior was beyond our ability to continue coping as his parents. We could not bring Mark back to our home, as much as we all wanted that. We had to find a new home for Mark.

After a lot more input from professionals, we decided to move Mark to the Devereux School in Victoria, Texas. We were reassured that—at the point we chose this facility in March 1967—the Devereux name had been associated with pioneering approaches to special-needs students for more than half a century. In 1906, Helena Devereux had been a young teacher hired to work in a South Philadelphia public school that served some of the city's poorest families. She was moved by the plight of her students, but especially those children with special needs who had little hope of growth within that school system. In stark contrast to the prevailing wisdom of the era, Helena was convinced that even children with significant disabilities could learn, *if* the environment was tailored to their needs. Public school officials soon saw the progress she was making with a few students and began clustering special-needs children in her classroom. In 1911, the title of Director of Special Education was created and offered to her by the Philadelphia Board of Education. However, Helena surprised school officials by turning down the job. These children needed a different kind of environment than what the public schools could offer. In effect, Helena believed, they needed a home. So, she began teaching some students in her own home, where they showed even more improvement. That strengthened her resolve. By 1918, she moved to a better facility—a house she rented in Devon, Pennsylvania, using her own savings to make the move. Helena and about a dozen students turned that new residence into their home. Eventually, she purchased the house she had been renting as well as a nearby estate. By 1922, her expanding programs were known as Devereux Schools. She reached as far as the West Coast with a 350-acre facility in Santa Barbara, California. Helena was still alive and involved with the organization when we moved Mark into the Texas home. She died in 1975 at her home in Devon at age 90.

The Victoria, Texas campus was one of the newest of the Devereux facilities and accepted residents aged 6 through young adult with mild to severe emotional, behavioral and/or learning disorders. For us, that long journey across Texas was emotionally as well as physically exhausting. Lillian and I had decided to take Kym and Jennifer along so that they could better comprehend this pending breach in our family. Fortunately, the Devereux staff provided for our lodging and took extraordinary steps to put us at ease. After a series of meetings to arrange for Mark's admission, we all went on a tour of the campus's two divisions that were separated by several miles.

Mark would be housed in the Ranch Unit. As we arrived at this facility, Lillian looked around and was visibly relieved. We all were pleased. Even the girls were caught up in the excitement of the wide expanse of grassland with rough-hewn fences housing a menagerie of farm and domestic animals. As we strolled through the ranch, I could see the dormitories were accommodating to the developmental limitations of the residents. Most importantly, we could see right away that Mark was pleased.

Throughout our orientation, staff members went out of their way to reassure us about their capacity to meet Mark's needs. They took seriously the Devereux ideal that this was a home where everyone was expected to interact in a cooperative way, almost like a family, even though clearly the staff was trained clinicians in charge of shaping the whole program.

As we got ready to leave, we were surprised to see Mark raising his hand to wave goodbye with a big grin on his face. We drove away with a prayer of praise to God who keeps His promises to watch over faithful families.

As the miles passed, Lillian and I each privately wondered: *Was this too good to be true?* As pleased as we were, nagging doubts kept surfacing in the days that followed. Had we made the right choice for our son? Had we handed off Mark's uncertain future to others in exchange for peace in our home? Was this a proper bargain for good parents to make?

Once we returned to Fort Bliss, periodic reports began arriving in the mail from Devereux. We opened each envelope with trembling hands. Our hearts were pounding as we tore the flap on that very first letter. We quickly scanned the basic facts at the opening of this report. We already knew that Mark had been experiencing "severe psychotic-like outbursts of temper." We knew that he was "moderately retarded and emotionally disturbed." We knew he had been placed in "special education ungraded classes" and was receiving "speech therapy."

What didn't we know? The report said: "Due to pronounced hand tremors, writing is not only difficult for Mark to produce but also for anyone to read. He is able to type and does most of his written assignments on the typewriter." Here was a fascinating insight: "The severity of hand tremors seems directly related to the degree of competency Mark feels in his assigned task, be it academic or manual."

We thought: Perhaps if he begins to settle into the Devereux routine and gain confidence, those tremors might not be such a daunting problem for him.

In fact, as we read further, we could see that he was adjusting: "Mark was programmed in a low-pressure combination tutorial-work-pre-vocational schedule. Within this setting he was able to perform adequately, to make good interpersonal associations, and demonstrated the ability to learn new routines and perform them well. ... Within his structured placement in the Ranch Unit, Mark was able to make a good initial adjustment. In this basically low-pressure, non-competitive program, Mark has interacted well with both peers and adults, although the latter was more difficult for him. He has both sought and accepted friendship with his peers. Initially, Mark would reject all offers of help or instruction. He tended to relate to all offers of assistance with: 'I know how.' However, this has diminished, and Mark can now accept assistance and instructions without feeling he is losing face."

One sure sign of his confidence was that the tremors were subsiding. "Considerable improvements are occurring in the use of tools and in Mark's ability to stay with a task long enough to learn it. Once he feels he can do it, the tremor noticeably diminishes, allowing him to perform more effectively."

We were relieved by the conclusion: "Mark has improved much in gross motor coordination, and is able to participate in ranch work, use a shovel, do exercises, etc. He does especially well in cement work, which he likes. He is learning good work habits. Mark has had a few tantrums recently; crying spells have not occurred for several weeks."

Lillian could not have been more pleased. She had dreaded receiving this first progress report. She had even imagined we would be summoned back to Victoria with instructions to find an alternative to Devereux. Now we both could get some relief from our daily anxieties about Mark.

For a while, our parental fears subsided. But, how could we not worry as we thought of our son each day? He was so far away. Then, months later, came the next report. Our hearts were pounding once again as we read the latest news.

Mark now was 13. "There have been no medical problems reported during this period." That was a relief! In Mark's academic program, "improvement is noted in concentration and attention span and in frustration tolerance." This was also good news, although the next line warned that these gains "remain fragile. Attitude toward achievement-oriented situations is such that Mark sets high goals for himself, thus becoming frustrated, exacerbating his tremor and causing him to become upset and unable to concentrate."

Our pride in our son soared as we read that the staff could see he had "a tremendous will to succeed." We knew that. Now, they knew it, too. This was a good sign.

Deeper in the report, we found the good news we had hoped to receive: "In learning situations outside the classroom Mark is eager, cooperative and tries very hard. He has continued to participate in various work projects such as fence-building and clearing land. The harder the job, the better Mark likes it. Mark's hands used to shake so badly he could not even handle a shovel, but he has persevered and now has mastered almost all hand tools. Improvements in general coordination are noted. ... There have been no violent temper outbursts recorded during this six-month reporting period."

Then, these lines startled us: "Interpersonal relationships continue to develop along positive lines. Mark seems to be the most-liked student at the ranch."

We read that a second time: "Mark seems to be the most-liked student at the ranch." We looked at each other. We said nothing. We continued reading. The report continued: "With his peer group, Mark is cooperative and appears comfortable as a member of the group. With adults, there have been noted gains in Mark's ability to accept advice and guidance; he no longer equates instructions with personal criticism. He relates more freely and is learning to relax in adult company."

We looked at each other, again. Relief was obvious on our faces, but we were so emotionally fragile ourselves when we thought about Mark. We took pains not to trigger further anxiety by even discussing the report. What could we say? Our Mark not only was learning and developing new skills—he was "the most-liked student at the ranch." That was a fact. The staff had reported it!

Lillian and I silently pondered this news. From the new perspective of our distance from Mark, I finally could see that Mark's journey, despite his disabilities, was a universal journey. All of us are searching for reassurance—for a home where we are loved and accepted. Although Lillian and I did not voice it that day, we shared in silent praise to God.

No, Mark was not with us. But Mark had found a home.

Even as our son was surprising us with his integration into the Devereux family, I was about to experience a different kind of integration. Shortly after returning to Fort Bliss, I received orders to attend the Command and General Staff College at Fort Leavenworth, Kansas. This is a prestigious graduate school reserved for the Army's brightest and best. The college had been established in 1881 by William Tecumseh Sherman after the Civil War when President U.S. Grant made him commanding general of the Army. By 1967, the school was known worldwide as an elite institution attended by leading captains and field-grade officers from the U.S. military as well as officers of equivalent levels from nations around the world. The alumni list was a Who's Who of famous officers, including Generals Dwight Eisenhower, Omar Bradley, Douglas MacArthur and George Marshall. The list of foreign countries who sent top leaders to the college included Ireland, Egypt, Lebanon, Pakistan, Argentina, Indonesia, many nations in Africa and all the countries of Scandinavia. My course would be a nine-month sabbatical for study with a fraternity of hand-picked, mid-level officers who were expected to become senior commanders and staff officers. Given the many advances in technology and strategy, students were expected to adapt to those changes as we played out roles and missions we might soon face. We were regarded as the next generation of commanders and staff officers who would be called upon to face future threats to the free world.

Having been selected to be a part of this august body was reward enough for me. An added bonus was the reunion with longtime friends and comrades-in-arms such as several West Point classmates as well as Bob Schneider and my University of Arizona confederates, Jim Dozier and George Loffert. Plus, I was soon to meet other promising officers, such as then-Maj. Colin Powell, the future Chairman of the Joint Chiefs of Staff and the Secretary of State.

This move was welcomed by Lillian. She liked the change of scenery, both physical and psychological. We both would miss John and Kate but we would be reunited with other friends. Lillian's reunion with Gloria and Judy was an emotionally charged event. Despite our lingering guilt over leaving Mark behind, we found ourselves buoyed by the new order in our household. For the first time in many years, Lillian could feel free, at a moment's notice, to accept invitations for tea and conversation with other women. Both of us could focus more on nurturing Kym and Jennifer. This was a major turning point in our lives.

Ironically, we shared this hopeful new outlook on life even as the Army was shoehorning us into some of the most spartan living conditions we had seen in years. "Student housing" was divided into five separate areas that ranged from a converted 19th-century cavalry barracks to individual cracker boxes. Although each area's architecture was different—there was no consensus on which was best. Each family had to weigh the pluses and minuses. Lillian was happy that we wound up with a unit in the converted barracks, called The Beehive. Those apartments had the most space among the five areas. The downside was the constant challenge of antiquated plumbing, oddly shaped windows, 24 steps up to our front door and the awareness that everyone living in that building was packed side by side—so close to each other that it really did feel like living in a hive! In contrast, the tiny houses in Pershing Park were separate dwellings, but they had half the floor space and fewer bedrooms.

In those first few days, we all joked about the challenges of such housing. At this point in our military careers, all the senior officers and our spouses assumed we had moved beyond such close quarters. There was a lot of the good-spirited joshing that helped to establish new friendships and strengthen old ones. Lillian, Gloria and Judy joyfully renewed their friendship, which had been abruptly put on hold after graduation in Arizona. As they tried to catch up on where they had left their relationship, Lillian told me she had a realization that their perceptions of each other had shifted. For the first time, she saw how far Gloria and Judy used to go out of their way to compensate for Mark's behavior—and to help allay our constant concern for Mark. With Mark happily adjusting to life at Devereux, Lillian discovered that she was more of a peer among friends than the source of their constant concern.

Not everyone chafed under the living conditions. Kym and Jennifer were thrilled that, for the first time in their lives, each had her own room. Kym unleashed a pent-up mania for posters. With some misgiving, Lillian and I began to recognize and appreciate this teenage assertiveness. We also wondered if we were paying a price for what must have seemed like our benign neglect of Kym as we focused so much of our energies on Mark.

I quickly learned how to succeed in this challenging new program. The crucial skill, each day, was: listening! The instructors were expert at giving us all the information we needed to know. Paying attention to what they emphasized in class was the key to success. This was not a case of rote memorization—far from it. The goal of the course was to show how well we could analyze and respond to new challenges. But these instructors were laying out all the essential principles we needed to master. Written examinations were heavily weighted to assure student retention of those precepts. Our reading assignments were frosting on the cake.

Our classroom exercises were simulations of real-world events. Team assignments took advantage of the mixture of branches and experiences of officers that made up each section. In our simulations, we had to respond to crises with Artillery, Armor, Infantry, Air Force and other resources. Foreign officers were integrated into exercises in cognizance of their nations' likely roles in actual conflicts. Students were chosen to present the teams' solutions and we subsequently were critiqued by faculty and fellow students. As students, we joked that each exercise had three solutions: the right solution, the wrong solution and the school solution. To their credit, our instructors did stress that the classroom solution was not necessarily the only valid solution.

The total enrollment of 1347 included 96 foreign officers from 51 countries. There were 37 black American officers—close to 3 percent of the student body. While that lagged behind the 12 percent of all Americans who were black at that time, I was impressed to see so many field-grade

African-American officers assembled in one place. At Fort Bliss, I had become accustomed to weeks passing by without seeing another black officer above the grade of captain.

The Command and Staff College was as close to successful integration as I had ever experienced in the American armed forces. There was no effort to cluster minorities in classes or housing. All families shopped in the Post Exchange and commissary. All children went to Post schools. With the exception of occasional individual jaunts into Kansas City, social activities were planned for the entire student body and centered around the Officers Club where everyone freely gathered. Our spiritual needs were serviced by the Post Protestant and Catholic chaplains. During the entire student year, I never encountered a single negative experience that turned on racial issues.

In a nation where race is such a defining factor, Lillian and I often talked about why there seemed to be no color bars cutting across that community.

I told her, "The Command and General Staff College is a career benchmark. Everyone entering this program assumes that the others have earned their slots. Whatever our individual stories, we all had to break into inner circles by demonstrating our abilities. Now, all that matters in this program is successful completion of the challenges we face, which requires teamwork. Everyone in this program knows that exploiting differences runs counter to our goals. Given these conditions, learning flourishes because we all want to get on with the business at hand. In this school, cooperation means success."

"It's the same on the home front," Lillian said. "Families face the same challenges. We all can see that too many people are crammed in too little living space. Those of us at home share the same complaint: Too many men preoccupied every waking hour with their college assignments. And, we share our pleasures. We enjoy the same amenities. Everyone is welcome everywhere and the ground rules in this temporary encampment are the same for everyone. There is no advantage to bias here—nothing to gain by it."

I observed something else. "We're also such a select bunch—so accomplished at this point in our lives—that there aren't any victims here," I said. "At least, there isn't anyone wanting to publicly acknowledge having been a victim. Color hasn't gone away as a dividing line—it's just that everyone has a vested interest in acting as if it has somehow faded into the background."

Lillian pondered this for a while, then a knowing smile spread across her face. "Hmmm," she said. "I wonder how all these enlightened people would act—" and she paused for dramatic effect "—if our children were of dating age?"

I smiled and nodded. A wise woman, indeed. Whether enlightened or acting on shared self-interest, I was impressed with that entire year—the first extended period of my life in which I couldn't discern a racial difference in our life together. Whatever the college had done to achieve this little miracle, it was a glimpse of a different kind of world that I hoped we all could enjoy in the future.

Another memorable milestone that year? I was promoted to lieutenant colonel on October 27, 1967.

Graduation brought about another global scattering of friends. Officers from foreign lands returned to their nations. Orders for U.S. officers blanketed major portions of the Free World. Many were sent directly to the Pentagon. In our final weeks at the college, we were invaded by real estate agents from metropolitan Washington, D.C. Some of my Leavenworth classmates actually purchased homes sight unseen, except for a few facts and photos on the agents' brochures. Many of them bought properties that stretched their buying power to the upper limits in the hope that rising home values would leave them with a profit at the end of their Pentagon tours.

I did not have that opportunity. I was headed for Vietnam.

Near Hue in the autumn of 1968, from left:
Major Ray Spence, me and Major Robert Brown.

A photographer caught me serving near Hue.

The 8-inch howitzer was the real workhorse of our Field Artillery Battalion. We also mounted the 175mm gun on the same chassis. This 8-inch howitzer could accurately reach a target 18 kilometers away. With the 175mm, our range was 30 kilometers, but the 175mm was not as accurate as the 8-inch.

15

Vietnam

*We knew what Vietnam had been like, and how we looked
and acted and talked and smelled. No one in America
did. Hollywood got it wrong every damned time.*

**Lt. Gen. Harold G. Moore and journalist Joseph
Galloway in *We Were Soldiers Once ... And Young***

*To generalize about war is like generalizing about peace.
Almost everything is true. Almost nothing is true.*

Tim O'Brien in *The Things They Carried*

You won't see *my* "story" of Vietnam in a movie or TV series. I'm not alone
in saying that. Among the 2.7 million American military personnel who
served in Vietnam between President Eisenhower's first deployment in
1955 and our last troops' departure in 1973—there are 2.7 million stories.
Young people ask veterans, today, "Can you tell me what it was like in
Vietnam?" Well, the truth is, there are too many things to say. While we
were there, our senses were overwhelmed. Our hearts are still too full, all
these years later.

What was it like in Vietnam?

I want to tell you about soldiers like me—so many of the men and
women—who were proud to serve. To this day, we continue to mourn the
deaths of 58,000 Americans on those battlefields fraught with horrific
uncertainties. Stories of proud service, mingled with sorrow at the overwhelming loss of life, are shared among countless Vietnam veterans.

Pride and sorrow are the twin legacies of many wars. I went to Vietnam
from the college founded by General Sherman, infamous as one of the
bloodiest commanders in history. But in December 1860, when he heard
that South Carolina had seceded from the Union, Sherman's reaction was:

"This country will be drenched in blood, and God only knows how it will end. It is all folly, madness, a crime against civilization. You people speak so lightly of war; you don't know what you're talking about. War is a terrible thing!"

When the Confederacy finally surrendered in the spring of 1865, Sherman's reaction was: "I confess, without shame, I am sick and tired of fighting. … It's only those who have never heard a shot, never heard the shriek and groans of the wounded and lacerated … who cry aloud for more blood, more vengeance, more desolation."

Not long before he established the college at Leavenworth, Sherman addressed graduates of the Michigan Military Academy in 1879 and summed up his hard-won wisdom in the three most famous words he ever spoke: "War is hell."

He certainly was not alone. Every day for the balance of his life, General Eisenhower mourned the more than 400,000 Americans who died or went missing in World War II. He was the president who told the world, "My country wants to be constructive, not destructive. It wants agreements, not wars, among nations."

I stepped into the baffling warfare in Vietnam, proud to follow in their footsteps of service. This was a debt I owed to Rep. John Dingell who believed in me so long ago. This was a debt I owed to West Point. This was my duty as an American soldier. This was my lot in the life I had chosen for myself and my family.

Because I would be away from home for a year, Lillian and I decided that El Paso was the ideal spot for our family, based on our earlier experiences at Fort Bliss. Despite the intense heat, the extremely low humidity made the summers bearable. The cost of living was low. We liked the proximity to Mexico. Schools were adequate and accessible. Fort Bliss amply provided for the necessities and amenities that Lillian would require for herself and the children. Even better, real estate speculators had recently overbuilt in the area, so rental rates were reasonable. We quickly found a place we could afford with a large backyard, appliances in mint condition and an elementary school just half a block away. At least, I was leaving for Vietnam knowing that Lillian and the girls were comfortably settled.

The U.S. Army's official message assigning graduates from the Leavenworth program to Vietnam was set in typical military shorthand:

Indiv will send msg ntfy to CGUSARV advising of ch in ETA
when trans scd are ch at transshpmt or stopover pt fol dprt fr
CONUS. Such msg WB given to CO of mil instl enr for xmsn.
An ex bag alw of 134 lbs personal eff auth to acmp each indiv
while tvl by acFort Cncr tvl of depn and shpmt of POV not
auth. Wear of the Army Green Uniform is rqr for indiv tvl in
unif in CONUS during winter season. Indiv will arr Vietnam
wearing khaki trousers and short sleeve shirt and will have in
poss basic rqr khaki unif, fatigues and combat boots. Army tan
and green unif opt. Dress unif not required. Summer civ clo
desirable for off duty wear. UP para 11 AR 40-562 plague imm
are rqr; tvl need not be delayed except for the first vaccine dose.
Indiv needing corr eye lenses WB equipped with mask protective
fld M17 and nec corr eye lenses prior to dprt fr CONUS. The
introduction, pur and poss of privately owned wpn is prohibited
in the Republic of Vietnam. For tvl costs to and PD at TDY sta
for sch tng only.

I went to Vietnam at the American tipping point. On January 26, 1968, Gen. William Westmoreland was quoted in *Time* magazine, declaring, "The Communists seem to have run out of steam." Then, at half past midnight on January 29, the Tet Offensive launched assaults all over the territory Americans thought we controlled. At 0245 that first morning, the U.S. Embassy in Saigon was attacked. What ensued was a period of chaos Americans remember, today, from the Pulitzer Prize-winning photograph of the chief of South Vietnam's national police using a Smith & Wesson revolver to kill a handcuffed Viet Cong prisoner in the streets of Saigon. By February 11-17, we recorded the highest American death toll during any week in the war: 543 Americans killed in action and 2,547 wounded. Walter Cronkite broadcast his famous TV special on Vietnam in which he urged Americans to end the war "not as victors, but as an honorable people who lived up to their pledge to defend democracy and did the best they could."

I descended into that eerie world on July 20, 1968, aboard a commercial flight under contract to the Army. As we approached Long Binh, South Vietnam, in all the comfort of a 1960s-style American airliner with full stewardess service, I could see exploding mortar and artillery shells out the window! More than fear, I thought: *This is surreal! I'm landing in luxury in the midst of a battlefield.* That disorientation only grew as we glided along the runway without incident. Soon, I was able to casually walk down the ramp and into an airport that looked no different than any big-city airport. People went about their business with no apparent anxiety or sense of urgency. I found a bus designated to transport arriving officers to the U.S. Army processing center and boarded with a promise that my bags soon would follow.

At that time, the duration for senior command assignments was usually six months. In that time, I spent six months successfully commanding the 1/83d, which was a XXIV Corps Artillery 175/8in. composite Battalion. During that time, the 1/83d provided artillery support for many combat missions in the northern part of South Vietnam, which was the Corps operational area. Because of a six-month rotation policy, I spent the second half of my year-long tour as the Corps Artillery Logistics Officer (S4). In that capacity, I coordinated and advised the Corps Artillery commander on logistics requirements.

That first battlefield assignment was a daunting task. We tried our best to maintain constant communication between the three firing batteries for which I was responsible. However, they often were deployed miles apart from each other, so they sometimes needed to operate autonomously. We could call in airborne support, if necessary. But that was not always possible. We often were in dangerous territory where the security perimeters around our firing positions were under assault. Other forces were supposed to secure those perimeters so our men could focus on the mission of the firing batteries, but the support troops sometimes were not enough. My men often found themselves having to provide artillery fire support while fending off attacks close at hand. Some days, chaos ensued due to the unpredictability of warfare. It was not always possible to keep in touch with each unit. Things went wrong. Deadly firefights broke out. That's why I'm proudest to say that, during my command, the 1/83d never lost a soldier.

Between my two assignments—on the battlefield and then as a logistics officer behind the lines—I sought like-minded officers, especially those who shared my values and whose work I could respect. When I found such men, we quickly formed working relationships that occasionally evolved into lifelong friendships. One of the men I came to admire was Dr. Joe Babb, a doctor from Ohio who was just shy of 30 when he landed in Vietnam as our new battalion surgeon.

My executive officer Maj. Ray Spence was responsible for this doctor who served as our chief medical officer, and Ray still vividly recalls Joe's first day with us. Joe was directed into Ray's office. "Unlike most medical doctors with whom I had previous contact, Dr. Babb didn't show any air of superiority," Ray told me recently. "He was about as down-to-earth as any Yankee I had ever met. He was unmarried and planned for a specialty in cardiology. Following a few minutes of small talk, during which he apologized for not being up on all the specifics of proper military courtesy, including the rules for properly wearing the uniform, I said, 'Doc, most of the doctors I've known in the past couldn't care less about how they looked in uniform or whether they themselves exercised any military courtesy. You aren't expected to become a Hessian, parade-ground martinet with spit-shined footgear and starched uniforms. Just put polish on the leather on a regular basis and wear clean uniforms and you'll get along fine. As the battalion XO, I oversee and coordinate the staff. In your case, that does not include trying to tell you how to take care of our troops from a medical standpoint. Welcome to the battalion and the war. I'll do my best to get you back home in one piece.'"

Joe faced a few crises at first. Some of the men tried to take advantage of him, playing on Joe's natural compassion for putting soldiers on sick call. But, Joe quickly was coached by Ray on how to become more savvy about Army life. Together, Joe and Ray soon weeded out the malingerers.

Soon, Joe's natural compassion extended beyond our troops. Many of the untold stories about our years in Vietnam involve the constant efforts by our personnel to aid the Vietnamese victims of the war. In Artillery, I remember many times that our shelling was limited to avoid areas where civilians lived, even when we knew enemy forces had moved right into those areas to avoid our fire. In the overall scope of the war's destructiveness, that might seem like a futile effort to reign in the devastation. In the end, some of those efforts bore little fruit. The point is that Joe—and many other Americans—went out of their way to preserve life in the midst of a conflict that was rapidly turning into a vision of Sherman's hell.

As I think back on Vietnam, I continue to be inspired by Dr. Joe Babb's transformation from a green Army surgeon into the force for good he became during his time in Vietnam. While writing this chapter, I reached out to Joe again after many years. On August 29, 2018, Joe sent me the following remembrance with a note that said my request had touched off a flood of memories. Like me, this is not a part of Joe's life that he was used to talking about with others. His note concluded, "Thank you for the privilege of contributing this story."

A week later, Joe died in an auto accident just shy of his 80th birthday. Only in reading his obituary did I learn that he had, indeed, become a top cardiologist after the war. I also learned that the awkward young surgeon who, at first, was so easily duped by soldiers playing on his compassion was, in fact, a remarkable physician. Before ever landing in Vietnam, he had been a Fulbright Scholar. He was a graduate of the prestigious Johns Hopkins Medical School and did his residency at Harvard Medical School. Back home again as a cardiologist, he became a pioneer, credited with having performed the first angioplasty in Connecticut. He eventually became one of the nation's leading heart specialists.

Even though Joe was green when he landed in Vietnam, I realize now that he came to us from a very promising career. Reading his obituary and notes from his friends in the autumn of 2018, I finally understand more about the passion Joe brought to making even a hellish corner of the earth a little better place for the people caught in that war. Here is what Joe wrote just a week before he died:

> Going to Vietnam in 1968-69, I knew I would have the privilege to assist our combat and support personnel in an environment filled with unusual and potentially deadly health issues. I had not anticipated the chance to interact with the civilian population. When our medical team added this kind work to our daily routines, we had no idea we would be reaching back into the Dark Ages to grapple with an outbreak of plague.
>
> Both the process of supplying medical care to military members and the health challenges we faced were different than in prior wars. Supervising active-duty sick call became a regular part of the rotation every morning. We were responsible for the

medical care of our four batteries: Headquarters Battery, Service Battery, Communications Battery, and Transportation Battery. Additionally, we provided service for nearby units that did not have other access to a battalion sick bay or a battalion surgeon. Assisting me were medics from the surrounding batteries. We also were responsible for a long list of other duties from overseeing malaria medication to animal control, especially combating the rat population.

Minor injuries, including cuts and sprains, were treated at the aid station while more serious injuries were referred to the nearest hospital. Battle injuries from the field were stabilized by medics and flown by Medical Evacuation helicopters (Med Evac or Dust-off) to the nearest hospital for treatment. Virtually none of the major battle injuries were treated at the battalion aid station, a vast change from the practice in World War II. This was made possible by the greater availability of helicopter transport and resulted in many limbs and lives saved.

We also were actively encouraged to help care for the native population, a program called Medical Civil Action Program (MEDCAP). That's what I did, once I had settled into my routine duties. Our headquarters unit was located about 20 clicks south of Hue. During the French Indochina era, the French had established a medical school in Hue and, along with that program, built a sizable teaching hospital in Hue. I asked two of my medics to visit the hospital with me. First, we stopped at the main administrative building, then we noticed a smaller building set away from the other hospital structures. That was the Hue infectious disease ward. It had about 70 beds, but only four nurses and no doctors. About 75 percent of the beds were filled with patients and most of the patients had between two and six family members in the bed with them, a cultural practice with the Vietnamese. I was introduced to the nurses working in this ramshackle structure. All spoke Vietnamese and French, neither of which I understood, but we managed to communicate in English and we all knew the universal medical terms. Our first priority was to repair the building, which had torn screens, plugged drains and grime everywhere we looked. The hospital personnel were delighted that we would help. I drove to MACV headquarters in Hue and asked them about providing more medication, IV fluid, sterile dressings and other supplies to support this effort. They agreed. That's how we started our MEDCAP effort at the Hue infectious disease ward.

We set up a routine in which two of my medics and I would drive up to the hospital several times each week after morning sick call was finished. The medics suggested they focus first on repairing the screens, unplugging the drains and cleaning up the ward as much as they could. We all agreed that our efforts would be pointless without improved onsite sanitation and freedom from disease-carrying insects. While the medics were doing that, I would make rounds with the nurse who could speak the most English and eventually the medics would join us. I quickly learned that routine laboratory tests were unavailable, except for bacteriological testing. I was horrified, but the fact that I could at least run bacteriological tests turned out to be a godsend.

Although I arrived with little awareness of the infectious diseases in this region—my education moved at light speed. We were caring for a large number of patients with low to moderate fevers and moderately prominent lymphadenopathy. Taking advantage of my only available lab test—bacteriology—I was shocked by the results! What I would have diagnosed routinely as viral influenza in the United States turned out, in many cases, to be bubonic fever, better known as the Black Death. As we investigated, we learned that the vector for bubonic fever is the rat flea, which can convey the bacteria to humans. Understanding the Vietnamese culture helped unravel the mystery. Families slept on rice mats spread across the floors of their homes. These houses were usually in the midst of extensive rice paddies, which also provided homes for the rats. When darkness fell, and the people went to sleep on the floor, rats often entered the quiet houses looking for food. In the process, rat fleas could reach humans and transmit Pasteurella pestis, the bacterium of the plague. Stumbling on this unexpected disease allowed our MEDCAP work to streamline our procedures. We learned that we could do a sterile lymph node aspiration and the resulting tests would rule in or out the P. pestis within 48 hours. If positive, we knew which antibiotic could quickly kill the bacteria and IV fluids would maintain the patient until fever and illness subsided. This is a perfect example of how our efforts had remarkable results in saving lives.

Then, we also became involved in visiting orphanages in Hue, where we treated children with diarrhea, fevers, sores and a wide range of other disorders. We also provided vaccines for the children, which gave them broad protection later in life.

That's not to say every treatment plan was a victory. We encountered other diseases that are uncommon in the U.S., but that could have been treated. However, in some of the locations where we encountered these patients and their advanced illnesses, there simply was no way to treat them. Too many men, women and children died of disease during the war.

To this day, I am proud that I had a chance to save the lives of many children and adults. The U.S. Army medics who shared in this work with me are to be highly, highly commended for their passion to duty and commitment to the health of others.

Like Joe and me, Vietnam veterans rarely talk about the war years. I am saddened by his passing and I am so glad that I asked him to share a part of our story. Americans hear a lot about the big battles and the war's tragic outcome, but we rarely hear these stories about compassionate assistance in the midst of the conflict. It's an unknown side of the war.

My last Vietnam story is also one Americans will never see in a Hollywood movie, but it remains one of my most indelible memories of Vietnam. That year, Billy Graham made his second visit to minister to

Americans serving in the war. He had toured military facilities in South Vietnam in 1966—then he came back for a week in late December 1968, ending his mission on Christmas Day.

When he first landed in Vietnam, Graham delivered a radio broadcast that was relayed by stations around the world. His description of the situation paralleled my own assessment on the day I first arrived, not long after Tet. Upon landing, Graham said: "We have just arrived in Saigon to spend the Christmas holidays with our troops. There is a vast difference between the Saigon of today and the Saigon I remember from two years ago. Terror has become a way of life here. ... In spite of mortar attacks, rockets, grenade-throwing and terrorism of various sorts, life goes on. ... Somehow the people have learned to live with shooting, bombing, rockets, terrorism and mortar shelling."

That's how it was. He was simply describing Saigon in 1968. At that time, Graham was criticized by anti-war protesters for his strong support of the war. The question of supporting or condemning the Vietnam War had even driven a wedge between Graham and his dear friend Dr. Martin Luther King Jr. for a time. But that debate between Christian leaders wasn't something I had the luxury of following as an officer serving on the ground. What I needed was hope—a vision of what we all could pray was possible in the years to come.

That's why I was so moved by Graham's Christmas Day sermon from Tan Son Nhut Air Base. As he spoke, some of the military air traffic whooshing through the skies around him occasionally drowned out his words. But I still recall the reverence with which our men and women listened that day.

Graham said: "I wonder today, as we look at the world, if everyone of us isn't conscious of the fact that somehow we have failed as a human race. We have the technology today to bring paradise to earth, but we cannot because of human failure. ... This is Christmas Day and Christmas is supposed to be a time of love, a time of peace. But we can see by the planes that are flying all about that we are far from peace. The world today is at war."

That same day, astronaut Frank Borman also broadcast to the world from his orbit around the moon and Graham echoed Borman's message. Graham told us: "I heard a wonderful thing—a prayer Frank Borman prayed from the moon today. Here's what he said, 'Give us, O God, the vision that can see thy love in the world in spite of human failure. Give us the faith to trust thy goodness in spite of our ignorance and weakness. And, show us what each one of us can do to set forward the coming of the day of universal peace. Amen.' I'm sure that's the prayer of every one of us on this Christmas Day here in Vietnam."

Graham was right. Borman was right.

During my year in Vietnam, any semblance of regular church attendance was out of the question—but I often found time to talk with our battalion chaplain. We regularly shared passages from the Bible that inspired us to carry on each day. Our favorite came from the second chapter of Isaiah:

> *He shall judge between the nations,*
> *and shall arbitrate for many peoples;*
> *they shall beat their swords into ploughshares,*
> *and their spears into pruning-hooks;*
> *nation shall not lift up sword against nation,*
> *neither shall they learn war any more.*

Cliff, Lillian and Jennifer with Undersecretary of the Army Ken BeLieu.

16

Sometimes I Feel Like a Motherless Child

O Lord, sometimes I feel like a motherless child—
A long ways from home,
A long ways from home.

Traditional African-American spiritual

My return from Vietnam seemed to be the start of a promising new chapter in our lives. I had come through one of the war's most devastating years without a physical scratch—and could proudly say there had been no casualties among the men under my command. I could see so clearly that God was good. My career was on the rise. I received orders to report to the Pentagon. Another promotion might be on the horizon. Lillian and I even felt God's guidance in the selection of the perfect home in Alexandria, Virginia. The blessings kept rolling in like ocean waves.

Strange as this may sound, my posting to the Pentagon initially sparked more anxiety than my departure for Vietnam. I had heard horror stories about life around Washington, D.C., especially the skyrocketing housing prices and the rising racial tensions. Over the years, racial pressures around Washington had pushed many families into racially aligned neighborhoods that further enflamed tensions. On paper, our new Alexandria school system was officially integrated in 1965, but that meant little until the consolidation of the high school in 1971. Today, anyone who has seen *Remember the Titans*, starring Denzel Washington, understands the powder keg that teenagers faced as all high school juniors and seniors from across Alexandria were sent to T.C. Williams High School in 1971. In the movie, Washington plays Herman Boone, the real-life black coach who was assigned to meld white and black players in this racially charged melting pot. T.C. Williams also was the setting where my daughter Kym's racial awareness blossomed. She auditioned and was asked to serve as a team flag bearer. She saw the drama unfold firsthand.

At that time, America was just barely beginning to grapple with racial bias in a constructive way after the urban rebellions of the 1960s. In 1971, *All in the Family* debuted on network TV, holding a comic mirror up to the face of entrenched bigotry. That year, Satchel Paige became the first Negro league baseball player inducted into the Baseball Hall of Fame. Despite those signs of enlightenment, racial tensions in Alexandria reached such a fever pitch that President Nixon told a national audience that the triumphant success of Coach Boone's Titans actually "saved the city of Alexandria."

As I pondered this move to Washington, D.C., I was thinking as always about advancing my career. I knew the conventional wisdom in the U.S. Army that a Pentagon tour enhanced one's chances of earning a general's star. I also was aware that many officers, even those who were career-minded, avoided the Pentagon at all costs. "Way too expensive to live there!" I was warned. "Too much bureaucracy!" And, "Too far removed from the real Army!" Lillian and I prayed about all of this but the die was cast by the Army.

My first discernible sign that I should welcome this move was the news that I would be working in the Office of the Chief of Research and Development (OCRD). The head of the OCRD, Lt. Gen. Austin Betts, was one of the most respected officers in that elite circle known as Direct Reporting to the Army Chief of Staff. I was given this opportunity because of my master's degree in mechanical engineering. The Army had carefully targeted my career path—through advanced schooling and my Vietnam posting—to prepare me for this future. My engineering research and my Artillery command experience made me a natural fit for this crucial challenge of ushering in the next wave of surface-to-surface cannon and missile artillery. My background gave me a valuable perspective in preparing successful plans and budget proposals to develop these systems.

This all made perfect sense to me as a blessing, a sure sign that my career was still in the ascent. Then, Lillian and I also were surprised by our providential success in finding a new home with solid schools for Kym and Jennifer. Mark would remain at Devereux.

As usual, our search for affordable housing began with prayer, but the speed of God's response was unexpected. We knew that Bob Schneider, my OCU mentor, had been assigned to the Pentagon. I called him and—given the horror stories we had heard about trying to find suitable housing—we were overwhelmed to learn that Bob knew about a perfect rental just a few blocks from his home. We would be neighbors again. The house far exceeded our expectations. It was priced within our budget and had three bedrooms, a large backyard, plus beautiful landscaping. Our prayers had been answered big time.

Lillian's greatest concern was the availability and quality of local schools. Once again, Gloria came to the rescue. She assured Lillian that Alexandria schools were among the best in the Washington area. Further investigation by Lillian confirmed Gloria's claim, so we immediately enrolled Kym and Jennifer.

Then, I received word that my father was seriously ill. On weekends, I flew to Detroit to be with him and Mom. There I met two of my cousins, Palmer Lee Jordan and Johnnie Reeves, for the first time. Later, they would become an integral part of my life. I was relieved to see the support of our extended family because my father was in an advanced stage of dementia. He needed to be surrounded by loving helpers. My father sadly passed on July 15, 1970.

For a while, my life revolved around those somber visits with the family in Detroit and my all-consuming Pentagon assignment. Simply going to work at the Pentagon, which is by far the world's largest office building, engaged all the senses. The 17 miles of corridors formed an endless labyrinth, because many of those halls led to hidden chambers and tightly secured areas. These passageways were lined with images of historic figures and events. We could enjoy the calm of the beautifully landscaped central gardens if we ever had a spare moment, but that was in stark contrast to the turmoil that roared through these offices as 26,000 people worked and often raced between assignments. The Pentagon had the critical mass of a small city. We faced a daily challenge just getting into and out of the building as we navigated across the ocean of parking lots. Leaving work often meant sitting in 5-mile-per-hour traffic. Although we lived in Alexandria, my commute was sometimes two hours each way!

Within the broad span of Army weapons systems development, I was assigned as the action officer for surface-to-surface artillery. My overriding responsibility was to receive, evaluate, and craft written responses to budget-related inquiries from the congressional committee that controlled funding for these systems. Sometimes, personal appearances at congressional offices were required. Among my most important assignments was working with a NATO panel charged with establishing a common plan for surface-to-surface artillery among the member nations. That required me to lead a U.S. delegation of experts that met quarterly at NATO headquarters in Brussels, Belgium. In those meetings, I found myself in an international mix of professionals who required simultaneous translators and links to secure global communication.

After two challenging years in OCRD, I received an unexplained call to report to Gen. Betts. Although there was no apparent reason for concern, I was uneasy because there was no scheduled meeting. As I entered the general's office, I realized this was not a routine visit. Betts began by commending me for a job well done and asked several questions unrelated to my expertise. The pressure subsided, but I was totally unprepared for what was to come. Betts asked if I would be interested in interviewing for an assignment as a military assistant to the Undersecretary of the Army. I knew nothing about the job, except that this would be a very influential posting.

"I'm honored to be working for you, sir, and I'm honored to be considered for this new assignment," I told Gen. Betts, trying to carefully balance my response.

"I hope you understand this is a once-in-a-lifetime opportunity," the general assured me. He started to describe the new job, stressing that I would be working in the highest echelons of the military, reporting directly to the No. 2 civilian in the U.S. Army.

"As I say, I have been honored to work for you ..." I began again. I was worried that a sign of eagerness to move to this new assignment might offend the general, but my anxiety was unnecessary.

"I've already scheduled your interview with the Undersecretary—tomorrow," Betts said.

I realized that Betts was not surprised at all by this news. In fact, he had been aggressively lobbying on my behalf. Without his strong recommendation, I would not have been in the running for this highly sought-after job.

The next day, I found myself in a reception area decked out with historic portraits befitting the tastes of a New England gentleman: Thaddeus Beal. Trying my best to conceal any anxiety, I finally was ushered into Beal's office, where he rose to greet me. This soft-spoken Undersecretary went out of his way to make me feel comfortable. He said he preferred to be called Ted, then asked polite questions about my family. I was impressed that he wanted to know about Mark's condition. Beal's sincere questioning was a sign to me that it would be good to work for such a compassionate man.

The next day, I received the good news. I had been selected to become the latest of the five authorized military assistants to the Undersecretary of the Army. Unbeknownst to me, this was happening as Beal was departing, making way for Kenneth BeLieu, a former Army colonel and Washington insider. His political resilience and staying power were confirmed by the unlikely fact that BeLieu had worked for President Kennedy and, now, he was continuing as President Nixon's Undersecretary of the Army. BeLieu was Beal's opposite. He was earthy, quick to laugh and had a swagger and charm that reminded me of Will Rogers. Ken moved and worked easily with elite as well as rough-edged military officers.

Col. Lewis Ashley, an infantry officer, was the senior military assistant and, as such, Ashley served as BeLieu's executive officer. The military assistants, myself included, reported directly to Ashley. Then, Col. Ashley asked me to prepare some talking points for Mr. BeLieu to use during a banquet appearance. The Undersecretary was so impressed that he asked me to serve as his speech writer, along with my other duties. Preparing those texts for BeLieu, who placed great value on personal connectedness, meant that I needed to learn a lot about him in a hurry. We quickly developed an extraordinary openness. Ashley was sometimes visibly uncomfortable with this special relationship but was boxed in because he wanted to please his boss.

I began accompanying the Undersecretary on high-profile visits to such places as Berlin, Seoul, Panama, as well as many military installations inside the U.S. In that era, BeLieu emerged as a key military liaison with the White House. I collaborated with BeLieu on responses to major milestones in that era, including the anti-war movement that staged ever-growing protests in Washington. Partly as a result of that public pressure, BeLieu was also involved in White House efforts to end the draft and move to an All-Volunteer Force (AVF). As early as 1967, Nixon had proposed this idea during his campaign. By the time I came on board, BeLieu was in the midst of turning this idea into national policy. He already had filed multiple internal research reports for the White House with titles like "Alternative Option for All-Volunteer Armed Force" and "Reform of Draft System Through Executive Action in Lieu of Legislation."

I worked closely with BeLieu on some of the documentation needed to end the draft and win final approval for the AVF. BeLieu's role later was documented in Bernard Rostker's history of that effort, titled, *I Want You! The Evolution of the All-Volunteer Force.* These days, that history is often distilled into shorthand, as if protesters swarmed the mall in Washington, D.C. and suddenly Nixon ended the draft. In fact, that effort took years of concerted efforts. Nixon had backed the idea since his campaign, but BeLieu was one of the chief architects of the change.

In the end, BeLieu and I left Washington in concert. His retirement coincided with my selection to attend the Industrial College of the Armed Forces (ICAF). One of my last official acts was to write the Undersecretary's departure speech. Usually, BeLieu used my scripts as a starting point, then went on to exercise his considerable talents as an off-the-cuff speaker. At his retirement, this was the first time I heard him follow the remarks I had prepared word for word. Perhaps he was too emotional to do otherwise—or our partnership had matured until I had anticipated exactly what he wanted to say that day. This had been one of my most effective working relationships.

As I left that office, I thought I felt God's winds blowing me onward toward a bright future. The ICAF was widely known in the military as affirmation that I was bound for what the ICAF called "senior leadership positions." The program's mission was to "produce strategic thinkers who possess in-depth expertise in the resources component of national security strategy." The U.S. Army's aim was to "educate, inform and influence national and international security communities." This was heady stuff. Coming from my historic efforts with the Undersecretary, I was about to dive deeply into critical security issues emerging around the world.

I assumed that I had little to worry about on the home front. Lillian and the girls would not need to move. The ICAF campus was located at Fort Lesley McNair on a peninsula between the Potomac and Anacostia Rivers in Washington, D.C.

What I had not anticipated was that, in early 1974, the military health-care system ended Mark's residency at Devereux. After seven years, he was coming home to us. Once again, we found ourselves anxiously opening an envelope from the Devereux staff.

We were relieved to read this summary of Mark's exit interview. His therapist wrote: "Mark came in tonight in a very happy, cheerful frame of mind. He immediately stated that he would be leaving Devereux soon and stated that he would be going to a job-training school in Alexandria, Virginia, and that he would learn to be a delivery boy and deliver things to people. Mark seemed the happiest tonight that I have seen him in quite some time. He seems to have a goal for the future. He seems to feel that now he can go to a job-training program and make further progress, and I agree with him. He has gone about as far as he can go here at Devereux. When he first came to Devereux, he had numerous emotional problems. He has outgrown all of these and, at the present time, he is emotionally well-adjusted. He still has mental retardation, but he has learned to live with this and to try to make the most of what abilities he does have."

Unfortunately, that Devereux progress report proved to be an overly rosy prediction of what would happen when Mark returned to our house-hold. Once again, Lillian faced the daunting challenge of attending to Mark's special needs while she was trying to cope with all the friction of parenting a smart and strong-willed teenage daughter. Before we moved to Washington, Kym had lived in mostly white neighborhoods surrounded by lots of other military families. At T.C. Williams, she found herself at the heart of the nation's continuing struggle over racial injustice. In those few years, both of us—father and daughter—were grappling with major forces of change in our American culture. Yet, looking back, I know that I intentionally left the major share of parenting to Lillian. For her part, Lillian encouraged that division of our roles. She preferred to shield me from a lot of what was unfolding each day. That was true even after Mark rejoined our family circle.

Kym thrived by building her own strong support system among friends and mentors, most of whom I did not know very well. As a student living in the center of the T.C. Williams drama, Kym quickly came down on the side of those working to overcome years of entrenched racism and injustice. I wish I had spent more time getting to know her friends and learning about how she saw the world changing all around her. We both were caught up in historic changes, yet we never found much time to talk about our separate worlds.

Then, there was Jennifer who was happy, successful and uncomplaining about the growing strains in our home. Her natural exuberance, which was heightened by the acquisition of Joshua, an Old English sheepdog, kept her focused on the joyous side of life.

Together, we found much to celebrate. I still fondly recall how thrilled we all were to learn that Kym was accepted by the University of Michigan.

Hindsight is so much clearer than what we can see in the midst of daily life! Now, I realize that my distance from the girls' lives made it easier for Lillian to channel my available family time in Mark's direction, once again. Lillian and I certainly needed help! Mark was landing on our doorstep after the glowing success at Devereux, including promises we felt obligated to turn into reality. To begin with, the happy equilibrium of daily life at Devereux had been yanked out from under him. His world was turning upside down. The heavy burden of trying to find placement for Mark fell disproportionately on Lillian's shoulders. When the search to make good on our hopes for vocational training and employment began to look futile, Mark began to regress.

My presence on the highly coveted list to attend ICAF was a clear affirmation of a bright career future. This would be a year long curriculum for "selected military and civilians for senior leadership positions at the post graduate, executive-level of study." ICAF objectives were:

- "Produce strategic thinkers who possess in depth expertise in the resources component of national security strategy."

- "Educate, inform, and influence national and international security communities with regard to evolving security resources management issues."

- "Be the nation's premier educational institution in the area of national security resources management."
- "Provide a program of joint professional military education that prepares graduates to operate in a joint and combined environment."

ICAF provided an assortment of enlightening and challenging experiences. The student body was made up of highly diversified senior military and civilian representatives from cabinet level departments. I was impressed that our group included a number of former POWs from Vietnam, which added a sobering awareness that our research into security issues were life-and-death matters in global conflicts.

The class was sectioned into industry study groups, each consisting of representation from the entire spectrum of executive departments. I was assigned to the Food Industry Group. In addition to the usual study, research and analysis of national security impact, the group was mentored by experts in the field. Associated instruction included a trip to the Campbell Foods Company in Camden, New Jersey. All industry groups employed the same methodology and rendered reports on their findings to the entire study body.

The ICAF experience was greatly enhanced by a broad spectrum of renowned guest speakers covering a wide ranging number of political, economic and social issues bearing on national security. The most memorable part of the ten months of study was the industry group visits to other nations to study national power concerns with emphasis on the resource component. Countries to be visited were grouped together into three nation groups. Students were allowed to indicate their desired destinations in order of preference. The final selection was based on a computer program called "The System of Least Regrets." I was given my second choice, which was Senegal, Ivory Coast, and Nigeria. There were nineteen members in my team led by an Air Force Brigadier General. Dakar, Senegal was the first stop. Upon landing at the airport, I was startled by the people servicing the terminal at all levels whose "blackness" shone in such stark contrast to what I was accustomed to seeing.

The French influence in Dakar and its surroundings was profoundly clear. Accommodations were less than spectacular but satisfactory. The group met with country leadership who gave a "State of the Nation" briefing and allowed ample time for questions. While touring the city, the group had their first exposure to the glaring contrasts that would characterize all three nations we would visit. There was no visible evidence of a middle class. There seemed to be only poor, rich and richer. People were both cordial and surprisingly cosmopolitan. A tour trip to Goree Island, which was a short boat ride from Dakar, exposed the dark side of the history of Senegal. It was there that the slave trade flourished. The island was the docking point where slaves were processed using unspeakably evil practices and loaded directly onto ships for transport to America. The shackles and other paraphernalia had been preserved as a horrific memorial.

The next stop was Abidjan, Ivory Coast. The gap between haves and have-nots was even more conspicuous than at Dakar. I stayed in a five star hotel that rivaled any seen in the states. Just beyond the edge of the hotel's lavishly appointment gardens were scenes of abject poverty clearly visible to patrons. Again, the Colonial French influence was keenly evident.

The last stop on the travel plan was Nigeria. Lagos, the capital city, was a bustling metropolis. People were everywhere and so were the manifestations of poverty. Open sewage channels ran parallel to the roadways. Unlike Senegal or the Ivory Coast, there was evidence of a fledgling middle class. The itinerary included meeting with the head of the Province of Lagos whose territorial jurisdiction was roughly equivalent to that of a U.S. Governor. After the usual briefing on national issues, time was set aside for questions. It had been noted by members of the ICAF group that despite the destitute conditions and the teeming streets, violent crime was not a prevailing problem. When asked for an explanation, the province head stated that while the West would not approve of their methods, they were well understood by the citizens and exceedingly deterrent. Whenever a perpetrator was caught in the commission of a crime of violence, he would be summarily taken to the city square and shot. So much for crime prevention, Nigerian style.

Other stops in Nigeria included the historic province of Benin and the University of Ibadan. Nowhere was evidence of negativity towards Americans more prevalent than at the university. There was an air of militancy not unlike that in American colleges and universities during the sixties.

I was a particularly vulnerable target for those who perceived American blacks as too submissive.

The only disappointment of the trip occurred when one member was stricken with malaria. He received good medical care but unfortunately, missed a significant portion of the journey.

When I got home from Africa, the whole family celebrated the news that I was promoted to full colonel, or "Full Bird Colonel" because the insignia is a silver eagle with wings outstretched.

On June 1974, after five years in Washington, D.C., we had to pack up once again and head to my new posting at the U.S. Army Field Artillery School at Fort Sill, Oklahoma. I was relieved when Lillian told me she was pleased about the move. She reasoned that Fort Sill would be a better environment for Mark. Jennifer seemed fine with the cross-country move. Kym was heading off to the University of Michigan, so we thought she would not be affected. With my promotion, Lillian assumed our new home would be comfortable. Her hopes were met when we got a look at the stately quarters on Leever Avenue that were reserved for officers at my new 0-6 level.

I was the new Chief of Studies, U.S. Army Field Artillery School, and would oversee the study and development of Artillery weapons systems. Everything seemed to be falling into place, once again. We found a spot for Mark working with local Goodwill Industries. He also was adopted by the Post Explorer Scouts. Jennifer rapidly made friends and said she was looking forward to her new school.

I reconnected with the Officers Christian Fellowship, the new name of the Officers Christian Union. This chapter was mentored by Gene Warr, an Oklahoma City businessman who had been instrumental in organizing and promoting several Billy Graham crusades. When I got involved in the group, Warr spiritually adopted me and we formed a strong personal relationship.

Lillian and I expected to face some challenges—and we did. The complex analysis of developing new systems was frustrating for me, because it often was difficult to judge whether we were making any progress. So, I was often heading to work in the morning already focused on the day ahead of me. Mark was not adjusting as we had hoped. As a result, he was becoming more contentious. These were problems, yes, but Lillian and I assured each other that these were simply bumps we would take in stride.

What I had not discerned, even after decades of marriage, was Lillian's iron will in her long-suffering role as the military wife meant she would never complain. If she was not feeling well, she would conceal her symptoms until the pain was unbearable. So, she quickly got my full attention when she revealed that she was experiencing numbness in her side and that her balance was erratic. The Post neurosurgeon was our next-door neighbor. We immediately got an appointment and a comprehensive evaluation. The doctor concluded the problem was pressure on her spine at neck level. He recommended corrective surgery. Then, he arranged for a second opinion from the University of Oklahoma Medical Center in Oklahoma City. That second doctor concurred and scheduled surgery at the Medical Center.

Lillian and I both were reassured by all the loving friends and relatives who soon surrounded us. Gene Warr stepped in with prayer support—and so much more. The commute between Fort Sill and the Medical Center was more than two hours each way. Gene and his wife, Irma, graciously welcomed me into their home throughout Lillian's hospitalization. I called my mother in Michigan to let her know about Lillian's condition and she in turn notified Aunt Ola who was the Florence Nightingale of the family. Aunt Ola immediately enlisted the aid of Aunt Veda, a nurse, and both flew to Fort Sill to be with Mark and Jenny until Lillian had sufficiently recovered from surgery.

After several hours of surgery, the doctor informed me that Lillian was paralyzed from the neck down and recommended that his team perform a second operation immediately. There appeared to be no other choice, so I consented. The second surgery was also unsuccessful. At this point, she was placed in the intensive care unit and the staff told me that there was nothing more the surgeons could do. We had to focus on her recovery, even with the paralysis.

Aunts Ola and Veda were taking care of Mark and Jenny, so I made my temporary base camp at the Warr's home and spent each day at Lillian's side. She could barely communicate with me, if at all, and I tried to imagine the agony she must be experiencing. I was also wrestling, hour after hour, with my own helplessness. As a man of action, my powerlessness was infuriating. I took comfort in the promise that God was truly our refuge and strength.

Periodically, I would check in with Ola and Veda. They would reassure that all was well at home and, through their prayers, they were in constant touch with the Great Physician. Even though it was difficult for Lillian to speak, she expressed her gratitude for all of this loving support, including visits to her bedside by Gene and Irma.

After several days of vigil in the Intensive Care Unit, I felt that I really should make a round trip back to Fort Sill to check on the family. I wanted to share the latest news face to face and, at the same time, ensure that Jennifer and Mark and the aunts all were holding up. Before I left Lillian that day, she managed a brief affirmation of faith: "He is able."

To this day, I regret how I handled this crisis. I have reflected on my choices many times. The crushing burden of Lillian's revelation left me so numb that I was clinging to her hand, to prayer and to our long-established patterns of parenting. We trusted in God. We were sure we could overcome every barrier we encountered. I always relied on a rational assessment of any crisis we faced. I followed the course we had set throughout our marriage.

As a father, I realize, I failed on multiple fronts. Mark and Jenny were aware their mother had been hospitalized, but I thought it was best to shelter them from the gravity of her condition. That's what Lillian and I had always done as parents. I had contacted Kym but advised her that all would be well. "It's not necessary for you to come home right now," I told her.

What I regret most is that I was at Fort Sill on that quick visit to shore up the home front when I got the call on February 26, 1975. A voice instructed: "Col. Worthy, we need you to return to the Medical Center immediately."

I sped to the hospital. When I finally reached the reception station, an aide whisked me into an empty room to await the arrival of the attending physician. His words fell like a sledgehammer: "I am deeply saddened to inform you that your wife expired this morning."

My legs would not support me. I fell to my knees. The rest of that day is a blur. I know that someone explained Lillian had stabilized in the ICU and had been moved to a ward to continue her recovery. Several hours later, she died of a massive brain hemorrhage. Lillian was only 47.

When I contacted Gene, he rushed to the hospital, too. Without any prompting from me, Gene responded to my emotional collapse by making all the necessary arrangements. He called his family's funeral director and set in motion Lillian's transport back to Detroit for services and burial.

That's when I began to see the impact of a lifetime of silently soldiering through our personal crises and assuming that our first duty as parents was to shelter the children. Mark was grief-stricken. My guilt really overcame me, though, when I drove to Jenny's school to pull her out of class and give her the news. I did not want to have this dreaded conversation inside her school. So, I asked the staff to inform her that I was outside waiting in the car.

I will always remember the jubilant look on her face when she spotted me in the car and bounded down the steps eager to greet me. I had never done anything like this. Her natural reaction to this surprising visit was boundless joy. Father had come for her.

I was dreading what I knew I had to tell her. I cannot even recall the words I spoke—only Jennifer's torrents of tears. She clung to me as if she would never let me go. Lillian's untimely death would have been devastating even if we had tried to prepare our children by bringing them to Lillian's bed in her final days. Instead, we had drawn a protective curtain around our mounting tragedy. Then, because we had concealed this awful truth, Lillian's death came like a lightning strike. I saw that so clearly in hindsight.

Even sitting there in our car—as Jennifer held me with all the strength she could muster—I thought of the telephone call I soon would have to place to Kym in Michigan. That burden of guilt at how I had failed to prepare my family was the hardest blow I ever felt in my life. The revelation of what I should have done—and what I now had to do—was as chastening as a refiner's fire.

As I expected, Kym did not hold back when she heard the news. I braced myself, but I could hardly take the resentment she unleashed. I knew she had to say her piece. I had to listen. Kym was furious at me. She also was furious that the hospital had moved her mother from the ICU to a ward where she was unable to signal her emergency. I was not even sure if Lillian had been conscious. I had no idea if she could have called for help. This was a medical tragedy. This was a failure within our family. This also was an injustice involving doctors who should not have transferred her from the ICU. Kym was sure we should have made a malpractice claim over Lillian's lax treatment. The anger flowed in all directions.

Just as I had fallen to my knees in the face of the initial news, I spent a lot more time on my knees in those bitter days. Not only was I utterly humbled, but I missed my Lillian with an agony that was palpable. How had this happened? How could we go on without her?

We flew back to Michigan for the funeral. The body had been shipped to the James Cole Funeral Home. Lillian's sister Alma, with assistance from my mother and other family members, planned for the funeral to be held at the First Baptist Institutional Church in Hamtramck, Michigan, on March 1, 1975. I was so grateful that the service paid tribute to Lillian by capturing the essence of who she was and the impact she had on the lives she touched.

Trying to atone for my failures in recent days, I decided I should take part in the service—a decision so painful that I regarded it as an act of repentance that might help us all with the healing process. Friends arrived from across the country to support us as a family. Bob and Gloria Schneider flew in from Alexandria, Virginia. Ann Blum also came from Alexandria. Peg Tanzer, the wife of my West Point classmate Jay Tanzer, came from Boston.

In the days that followed, the larger family convened. The consensus was that we should find a home for Mark in Detroit, where extended family could be more supportive. Our goal was to minimize the traumas for a motherless child with exceptional disabilities. My cousin Constance Baldwin, our resident expert on social services, agreed to help us find such a place. Her search led to a tireless advocate for the disabled: Eddie Mae Jones. Then, Mrs. Jones referred us to Thedoshia Carter, a group home provider. I am convinced that the hand of God was once again moving through this contact with Mrs. Carter. When I saw the wonderful relationships she had with her residents, I felt confident that Mrs. Carter could spread her wings further to serve as Mark's new maternal pillar.

The entire "village" was rising up to surround us once again. It was obvious to those around me that I was stumbling through these decisions in the wake of Lillian's death. So many people stepped up to help us through this part of our journey that I cannot even recall all the names.

Although I did not fully understand it immediately, the truth became clearer with each passing day and each kindness from a loved one: As a motherless family, we were homeward bound.

Mildred with Mark.

Mildred with my Mother.

17

Homeward Bound

Do not let your hearts be troubled. …
My Father's house has many rooms.

John 14:1-2

Maybe there's a chance for me to go back there
Now that I have some direction.
It would sure be nice to be back home
Where there's love and affection.

The Wiz

In the end, we all went home. The blessing for us was that we had family waiting there with arms wide open.

For a while after Lillian's funeral, Jenny and I lived at Fort Sill. Kym returned to her studies at the University of Michigan. However, I knew that I was facing a life-altering decision. As a single parent with a highly fluid career, I asked myself: *Can I meet the challenges of raising a 14-year-old daughter traumatized by having her mother snatched away without warning?* While I was comfortable with the arrangements we had made for Mark, I could not be sure of the long-term effects of physical and emotional separation from the only family he had ever known. After much contemplation and prayer, I decided we had to go home.

I requested a transfer to the U.S. Army Tank and Automotive Command (TACOM), an Ordnance branch facility in Warren, Michigan, to be near family. I was keenly aware that, by leaving my Artillery branch, I was closing the door on my aspiration of someday earning a general's star. I concluded that at age 47, I was young enough to pursue a second career. So, I decided to retire the following year.

I received orders to report to Warren on July 15, 1975. I was assigned as TACOM's Weapons Systems Management director. My duties encompassed development, engineering, procurement, quality assurance and supply and maintenance management of Army tank and automotive systems. To carry out this work, I had a support staff of about 100. Because it was a position usually assigned to Ordnance officers, I had a lot of catching up to do. It was a fresh and exciting challenge.

I was given housing in historic and spacious quarters located on the site of Selfridge Air National Guard Base near Mt. Clemens, Michigan. This was an altogether charming setting with beautifully manicured grounds a short walk to Lake St. Clair. Even the garage was heated. Jennifer and I saw that we had more than enough room for my mother to move in with us. Among our neighbors were Ed and Peggy Weathers with whom we had shared a duplex at Fort Sill years earlier and were among our closest friends. Despite the lack of Artillerymen around for company, my work was purposeful and fulfilling. Headquartered in Warren, Michigan, I was able to reconnect and spend time with extended family. I also discovered that my cousins Albert Sandifer and Janet McCurry were employed at TACOM.

Mark was faring well at Mrs. Carter's and Kym was forging ahead at U of M in Ann Arbor. Jenny was enrolled at Mt. Clemens High School. Even though she was uncharacteristically moody as she continued to mourn the loss of her mother, she seemed to be on a solid course.

I was now in position to reestablish my Detroit bearings and lay the foundation for retirement the following year. Early in 1976, I began to explore post-retirement employment opportunities. One of my job interviews took me to RCA in Moorestown, New Jersey. On my way back, I stopped in nearby Wilmington, Delaware, to visit my cousin Inez Wilson. It was there that I met a Wilmington school teacher who also was my cousin's landlady, Mildred Jackson. Sparks flew between us and, only after we met, Inez admitted she had planned this fateful encounter. Mildred had been widowed several years earlier. The RCA job never worked out, but I kept thinking of Mildred as I made my way back to Michigan.

After I filed my official request, the U.S. Army placed me on the retirement list on June 1, 1976. At that point, I had already accepted a position with General Motors commencing the first of July. This left me free to search for a new home. With help from my cousin Thelma Scott I scoured the housing market in the Detroit area, focusing on good school districts. The family's collective verdict was that I should buy a comfortable Cape Cod-style home in Southfield's Washington Heights subdivision. The house was a perfect fit. There was a master bedroom, a room for Mom, a room for the girls to share when Kym was home and a den that would be used as a bedroom for Mark whenever he was home.

My hopes were fulfilled as Jenny soon began to thrive at Southfield High School where she also competed on the cross-country team and joined a drama group. At the University of Michigan, Kym also was well on her way. Mark enjoyed coming home on weekends but occasionally balked at returning to his "other home." After a period of adjustment, Mrs. Carter suggested that he not make these weekend trips, because she saw signs that he was developing his own confidence and independence while living with her. Moving between two homes was too confusing, she told me. So, we discontinued those regular weekend visits.

For the first nine months of my employment at GM, I was an employee in training. During that time, I was exposed to engineering, (space) manufacturing and procurement. After that period, I was assigned to several posts with Chevrolet, Pontiac and GM Canada (CPC). Now, I was exposed to a different command structure. My various postings included supervisor of Truck Production Control and Scheduling as well as senior administrator CPC Group Quality and CPC Product Investigations. During my 14 years with GM, I served with many remarkable people but I am privileged to count three men among the most outstanding mentors and human beings I have ever known: Robert Hutchison, Dennis Madigan and Ivar Carlson.

Mildred and I kept in touch for more than a year before I decided to visit her in Wilmington, Delaware, where we finally scheduled a dinner at the Columbus Inn on June 10, 1977. This was our first date and my first of 20 visits to Wilmington over the next two years. Mildred came to see me in Michigan for the first time on July 29, 1977, her first of 29 visits to the Detroit area. Clearly, this was much more than a casual relationship. It had been gathering steam for an extended period of time under the trying conditions of distance and calendar management. It took a lot of love to make it happen, and we finally were married on August 4, 1979.

The wedding was in Wilmington at the Silverbrook United Methodist Church officiated by the Rev. Benjamin Hutchens and the Rev. O'Connell Osbourne. It was a beautiful and solemn union that began a new chapter in our lives. Both Kym and Jenny were able to attend.

1979 was a banner year! Mildred and I were married and Mildred moved from Wilmington to our new home in Southfield. Kym graduated from the University of Michigan. Jenny graduated from Southfield High School.

My Mother's Story

In 1986, the cruel subtleties of dementia began to emerge in Mom's interactions with us. I was still working at GM and Mildred was substitute teaching. Kym and Jenny had moved into their own apartments. Looking back, we could identify telltale signs that Mom's memory was failing, but the first significant warning signs of her disorientation were phone calls to my office. Neighbors called to let me know that Mom had locked herself out of the house. The greater danger was that Mom had been a terrific cook all her life and she was drawn to the kitchen. We were worried by her tendency to start a project, then forget that she turned on the stove or some other appliance.

After agonizing deliberation with the family, and a whole lot of prayer, we concluded in 1990 that it was best to find a place where she would receive the watchful care that she needed. Upon the advice of Eddie Mae Jones, who had referred us to the Carter home for Mark, Mom moved to the Hannan House, a residence for semi-independent seniors. Unfortunately, she began to exhibit troubling behavior that the Hannan House staff was not equipped to monitor. We had to move her to the Boulevard Temple Retirement Home, affiliated with the United Methodist Church and situated not far from Detroit's New Center.

During all of this upheaval, she never complained and maintained her sweet spirit. Too soon, it became time to employ hospice services. On June 28, 2001—while in the company of myself, Ola, Mildred, her nephew Tom Hollingshed and niece Barbara Jackson—she peacefully went home to be with God. She was 98 years old.

Jennifer's Story

After graduating from high school with high academic standing, Jennifer decided to accept the University of Notre Dame's offer to fly her to South Bend for an interview. Her decision to enroll at Notre Dame was partially prompted by the fact that my cousin Dr. Joseph Scott was a tenured professor. She graduated in 1984 with a major in psychology.

Ever since she was young, Jennifer's faith has shaped her life, including her compassion for the plight of others. Her lifelong devotion to her brother, Mark, certainly attests to the depth of her Christian faith. Over the years, she has worked for a number of companies, including in the human resources department of a steel company. However, her real passions have been music, writing and global activism. In 2004, a book of her poems, *The Potter's Wheel*, was published. In 2006, she performed a one-woman show featuring recitations of her poetry and a piano rendition of her own composition dedicated to her niece Anastasia. Jennifer continues to champion causes for the hurting and the helpless. When she learned of the abhorrent practice of human trafficking and abasement of African women, she became part of a missionary movement to combat these evils. Her mission work has taken her to Italy and Spain.

Mark's Story

The first four or five years for Mark at the Carter home were uneventful. We saw him often and he settled comfortably into the community. However, in late 1981, we began stumbling with Mark through a painful journey that is familiar to many families with special needs adults. Mark became restless and irritated at the Carter home and this frustration triggered his temper. When his tantrums became too serious to remain at that home, we found ourselves beginning a three-year cycle of outbursts and institutional placements. At one point, he wound up at the Detroit General Hospital Crisis Center, then he was sent to the Northville Regional Psychiatric Hospital. To this day, families in Michigan still tell stories of the deplorable conditions at Northville before it was finally shut down. Mark's move from the Detroit hospital to that Northville facility resulted in yet another move to a psychiatric hospital in Ferndale. The various medical reports that stacked up detailed Mark's hallucinations and delusions coupled with anxiety disorder. It is no wonder Mark's anxiety spiked in such a tragic merry-go-round! People were pushing, pulling and prodding him in bewildering directions.

At one point in this long journey, he did return to the Carter home—then another incident bounced him back to the Ferndale facility. In March 1982, Michigan Protection & Advocacy Services got involved in trying to find a residential setting for Mark. Our larger family was involved throughout this process, of course. We collectively discovered a hard truth that many other families had discovered before us: Michigan has a critical shortage of facilities to serve adults with the kinds of serious issues Mark faced. At one point, I wound up writing to U.S. representatives from Michigan asking for help. Persistence paid off and finally I found professionals willing to help us. However, we still faced a couple of years of cycling through the system before the summer of 1984, when Mark finally moved into a home in Leonard, Michigan. We were told that this new home was built with Mark's needs in mind. That autumn, I got a letter of apology from the Macomb Oakland Regional Center expressing regret that Mark's placement had taken so long. I thought: *How many other families are caught in this same traumatic cycle, still waiting for answers?*

We were relieved that Mark had found a good home in Leonard. He was able to settle in and make a life for himself, including new friendships. Over the years, he attained enough balance in his daily life that he could work in several workshops.

Despite all the tragic hurdles he faced throughout his life, what truly defined Mark's character was his faith, his love of family and his love of country. Mark refused to think of himself as a victim, because his faith in God was so strong that he was confident God would never make a mistake. He was a robust Christian witness and a true prayer warrior. No family gathering was complete without a prayer led by Mark. We would join hands and his prayer petitions were often punctuated with an entreaty to the Holy Spirit: "Give me faith!" There was no pretense in his style of prayer. It was his signature in our family.

He loved any opportunity to be with us. Family members still recall his eagerness to take part, to listen and to enthusiastically express his pride in our successes. He adored his sisters and his joy was obvious any time he was around them.

Patriotism also ran deep in Mark's spirit. He seized any invitation to sing the national anthem. At one point, he became convinced that he should enlist in the armed forces. This was such a strong and persistent desire that those around him had to assure him that the Army was aware of his interest—and he would be called, if he was needed.

We were thrilled when a softball team called the Over-the-Hill Bunch, made up of middle-aged men who had never lost their zeal for competition, welcomed Mark. He was proud of his softball team—and we delighted in that opportunity.

In his late 50s, Mark had a series of physical setbacks due to various conditions that emerged including extreme arthritis and high blood pressure. He died at the home he loved a day prior to his 59th birthday. To remember Mark, the staff of that home in Leonard arranged to have a tree planted and dedicated in his honor.

At his funeral, the Over-the-Hill Bunch added to Mark's eulogies. They also installed a bench in his honor at the Romeo, Michigan Recreation Center ball park. The inscription reads:

IN MEMORY OF
MARK WORTHY
AND HIS LOVE FOR THE GAME

ROMEO'S ANGEL IN THE OUTFIELD

1955—2014

Kym's Story

People around the world have followed Kym's courageous career. She is Michigan's Wayne County prosecutor, the first African-American woman ever elected to head that enormous office in southeast Michigan.

Before she took over, the department was often overwhelmed. In 2009, when Kym discovered more than 11,300 untested rape kits in a warehouse, she launched a campaign to analyze this evidence. In 2018, HBO broadcast a documentary, *I Am Evidence*, produced by Mariska Hargitay, the co-star of the TV series *Law & Order: Special Victims Unit*. Before the HBO debut of the film, Kym appeared with Hargitay in Detroit at an event to shine a spotlight on what the *Detroit Free Press* described as "the national trend of untested rape kits that stretches coast to coast." Kym's campaign to bring justice to victims of sexual assault continues. She was invited to talk about this ongoing problem across the U.S. in the prestigious series of nonprofit TED Talks. Her talk was broadcast in September 2018.

Kym is used to the glare of the spotlight. A decade ago, she wound up in international news reports for leading the prosecution of then Detroit Mayor Kwame Kilpatrick. This was a complex case that involved misuse of office, perjury and a long list of other felonies. Federal charges of extortion

Kym Worthy.

and bribery eventually were added. Dozens of other incidents and legal maneuvers erupted over the next few years before Kilpatrick finally wound up in federal prison at Fort Dix, New Jersey.

I'm proud that Kym grew up both brilliant and tough enough to go toe to toe with the most deeply entrenched crooks. I'm proud that she is carrying on that vocation of service to our country—part of the motto that has shaped my own life since West Point.

Like the rest of us in this vast Worthy village, family is a central pillar in Kym's life. She has three daughters: Anastasia and twins, Alessandra and Anniston.

Mildred's Story

As I enter my 90s and I look back across my life, my four decades of life with Mildred represents a lion's share of our family life.

We began our relationship with the sparks of what became a deep and abiding love. We were brought together partly by our shared experience of having lost a soul mate. A fatal blood clot claimed her first husband in the prime of his life. Somehow, across a distant geographic reach, we were brought together. Mildred and I are convinced that we would not have met, and our relationship would not have flourished, without Divine intervention. We needed God and each other to reclaim dreams deferred. Now, together by God's grace, we could rise up out of the ashes of despair.

Mildred's winsome personality enabled her to quickly reconcile relationships with members of my family after moving from Wilmington to our home in Southfield. She coped well with the usual tensions that arise under such circumstances. She carefully set about restructuring her life to accommodate the individuality of others without losing her identity.

From the beginning of our marriage, Mark called Mildred "Mom." This gesture was precious to her and did much to soothe anxious moments. She became one of three maternal figures undergirding his life, along with Lillian and Mrs. Carter. Mildred became Mark's nurturer, counselor, relentless intercessor and a strong link in the chain of support so vital

Mildred Worthy.

to Mark's development. She taught him the basics of penmanship and drilled him continuously to overcome his resistance to taking on tasks requiring fine motor skills. She celebrated his victories with him, inch by inch.

After a brief hiatus to get her bearings and connect with her professional colleagues, Mildred decided to resume her career as an educator in the Southfield school system. After Mom became a resident of Hannan House, we moved from Southfield to a condominium in Michigan's Bloomfield Township. We decided that we no longer needed the big house for just the two of us. Mildred continued to maintain her ties to the Southfield school system.

The Bible tells us to discover and exercise the gifts we have been given. Among the biblical list is helping and I have never seen a more vivid illustration of that gift than Mildred's tireless assistance to others. Nowhere was this more evident than in the case of Betty Lockett, the wife of my cousin Dr. Harold Lockett. Betty had been stricken with incurable cancer. Mildred frequently traveled to Ann Arbor, Michigan, to look after her when Harold could not be there. Later she would journey to Boulevard Temple to care for my mother. She washed her clothes, purchased new clothing as needed, periodically prepared and served meals, and advocated for her in general to assure that she was getting the kind of care she required. These and other acts of kindness and compassion were extended to my cousin Thelma Scott during her husband, William Scott's, illness and following his demise. She worked tirelessly with Thelma's daughter, Carol, to secure adequate housing for Thelma when it became necessary for her to move to assisted living. Mildred also found time to tutor Delvon Ellis, Barbara Jackson's grandson, during critical middle-school years.

For Mildred, giving is seamless and without boundaries. Once committed, she keeps on giving. Her "give now and ask questions later" approach to compassion became a healthy counterbalance to my more measured style in meeting the needs of others.

Mildred continues to be deeply engaged in the work of many faith-based agencies such as Youth for Christ and Angel's Place, a nonprofit organization providing homes and services to persons with developmental disabilities. She has served in multiple capacities at the Highland Park Baptist Church located in Southfield, including two terms as deaconess. Her long list of volunteer commitments also has included programs to raise scholarship money for needy students and networks to promote a wide range of women's issues.

Strengthened by Mildred's ever-growing vision of family and community connections, I gained a new perspective on the future of our collective journey.

The Story of the Village Continues

I opened this memoir with these words: "I am not the product of privilege, but I am from solid stock. The values flowing through my ancestral bloodstream are biblically based and, most likely, you will find they are values that flow through your family as well."

My first memories were of all these marvelous, vibrant, loving men and women who formed the village for me. The second chapter of my story began: "When I was born, I was wrapped in the dream of my proud relatives." While it was true that they originally dreamed of my success as a doctor—the truth is that the family encouraged me throughout my long career in the military and then with General Motors. From the beginning, I knew this truth: "I was raised by a village—and simply assumed that's how life should be."

As I look across the vast village that is my family, I have no precise accounting of our numbers, except to say: We number in the hundreds and perhaps in the thousands! My maternal great-grandparents were slaves who were given the names of Paton and Patsy Colbert. The branches of their tree are vast. To date, I have not seen a genealogical chart that encompasses the many branches from that generation of my ancestors. However, I do know that, as of 2006, my mother and all 12 of her siblings had passed away leaving 49 in my generation of first cousins. We have well over 100 offspring from my generation. I am not even trying to count our collective grandchildren and great-grandchildren. As of 2007, my father and all nine of his siblings had died, leaving 41 first cousins in my generation on that side of the family. A full accounting of this clan today is way beyond my reach.

In recounting my life, I have tried to hold up the signposts through which I believe I saw the movement of the Spirit. At West Point, a commitment to "Duty, Honor and Country" was instilled so completely in my life that I see these values echoing in future generations. I can never forget Mark's proud renditions of the national anthem.

I hope that you welcome my honesty in explaining how powerful faith has been a part of this journey. Life's best plans are interrupted, time and again by doorways that suddenly slam shut—or swing open. My advice throughout this story has been: Be prepared to spring forward. Always look for new frontiers. But, as you do, cling tightly to whatever pillars rest on the true bedrock in your life.

I am profoundly grateful for the United States Military Academy at West Point for enabling the chronicling of the pages herein and equipping this Black Knight to become a member of this hallowed fraternity and bear witness to the God given might of Duty, Honor, Country.

I leave you with Proverbs 3:5-6:

> *Trust in the Lord with all your heart,*
> *and do not rely on your own insight.*
> *In all your ways acknowledge Him,*
> *and he will make straight your paths.*

In Memory of
Mark Worthy
and his love for the game,
"Romeo's Angel in the Outfield"
1955 - 2014

The Over-the-Hill Bunch posed for a team photo. Mark
was demonstrating his military salute in the back row.

Walter Oehrlein and Cliff Worthy.

Acknowledgments

More difficult than writing this book is paying fitting tribute to those who helped me along the way. First, I need to thank Mildred, who has been a prime mover supporting this long project, including welcoming the brigade of advocates who helped me to stay the course all the way to publication.

My children, Kym and Jennifer, and my granddaughters—Anastasia, Alessandra and Anniston—were a constant source of support and encouragement.

Walter Oehrlein and Al Tochet worked tirelessly to make my dream a reality. Bob Toohey provided legal coaching and experiential assistance. Walter, my esteemed friend and fellow West Pointer, gave of himself in too many ways for me to try to detail his efforts. He was determined that *The Black Knight* would be published and was a guiding light throughout this journey. For his insightful counsel and selfless attention to the many details of this project, I am profoundly grateful.

Also, I am deeply grateful for the assistance—both literary and corroborative—of my West Point classmate the Rev. Dr. Robert W. Blum. Lori Costantini's insightful review of the manuscript was most helpful. Brian Palmer provided invaluable editing and comment as did Tom Watkins. In addition, I need to recognize Dean Hamm, Eric Sprague, Jeremy Salo, Linda Santo, Peter Bishop and Jaclyn Seikel for their technical expertise.

I'm also deeply appreciative of the Cedarbrook living environment, as it was so conducive to the fruition of *The Black Knight*.

Finally, I am grateful to the many Michigan-based organizations whose ultimate cause is to serve people with special needs—far too many individuals and organizations to name each one. I hope that all who I have described in this general way know that I remain thankful and hold all of you in my prayers.

At the risk of forgetting some, I do want to name, in particular, the staff surrounding the Dequindre home where Mark lived for so many years and also the wonderfully big-hearted guys of the Over-the-Hill Bunch. Your acceptance of Mark was a crowning achievement in his life and we welcomed your presence, too, at his funeral service. You may never win the highest awards in the world of softball, but your compassionate spirit ranks you among the great heroes in our story.

I have been privileged to serve as a director on the boards of a variety of nonprofits working to improve life for the disabled and functionally limited. These include:

Angels' Place
Hancock Residential Center
Recording for the Blind
Services to Enhance Potential
Westside Citizens for Retarded
Widman Foundation
Detroit Youth for Christ
Highland Park Baptist Church

CPSIA information can be obtained
at www.ICGtesting.com
Printed in the USA
BVHW031143280219
541437BV00002B/10/P

9 781641 800372